A Burroughs
Compendium

A Burroughs

interviews, memories and transmissions from
John Tytell, Douglas Brinkley, Lee Ranaldo, Ron Whitehead,
Tariq Zayid & Dee, rlmar, Allen Ginsberg & Neil Hennessy

photographs from
Chris Felver, Jon Blumb, Mellon, Gordon Ball,
Allen Ginsberg & Lee Ranaldo

edited by
Denis Mahoney, Richard L. Martin and Ron Whitehead

Compendium:

Calling the Toads

fringecore
beyond transgression

Ring Tarigh

Supporting a global literary community

the literary renaissance

a non-profit corporation louisville, kentucky

HOZOMEEN
press

1998
ANTWERPEN - WESTERLY - MYSTIC - LOUISVILLE

First Printing, April 1998
Copyright © 1998 to the authors and photographers.

book design by hozomeen press
cover & frontispiece photographs by Jon Blumb
back cover photos by Lee Ranaldo
cover assemblage::rlmar

NORTH AMERICAN DISTRIBUTION:
Ring Tarigh
P.O. Box 1345, Watch Hill, Rhode Island 02891
www.riconnect.com/ringtarigh

EUROPEAN DISTRIBUTION:
Fringecore
P.O. Box 165, 2600 Berchem 1, Belgium
www.fringecore.com

DIGITAL DISSEMNINATION:
Hozomeen Press
P.O. Box 174, Mystic, Connecticut 06355
www.boylancolor.com/palaz

LINKAGE:
the literary renaissance
1387 Lexington Road, Louisville, Kentucky 40206

ISBN 0-9659826-0-2

printed in the united states of america

Table of Contents

the West End, 1973   photograph copyright © 1998 Mellon

HELLO, MR. NICE GUY

by John Tytell

I met William Burroughs in the spring of 1974. El Hombre Invisible had recently returned to this country after more than two decades of self-imposed exile and was living in what he called "the Bunker," a cavernous space on the Manhattan Bowery with few windows and little outside light.

I had published an essay full of praise for NAKED LUNCH in THE AMERICAN SCHOLAR, a conservative establishment magazine. Although by reputation Burroughs was supposed to be glacial, I wanted to interview him for NAKED ANGELS, the book I was writing on the Beats, and I was nervous about it.

Burroughs' manner didn't help. He was diffident, laconic, punctiliously self contained and cool as a knife blade. He stared right past me into a middle distance, and he had little patience for small talk.

I felt a crusty brittleness, it might have been a residual class affectation, that reminded me of T.S. Eliot, and he told me he had seen Eliot who was in residence at Harvard when Burroughs was an undergraduate there. There was a dry irritated edge to his tone, he kept punctuating my queries with an impatient "next!".

He seemed much less interested in the past than in the present, and I recalled that in the "Atrophied Preface" at the end of his masterpiece, NAKED LUNCH, he had suggested that he was trying to write without memory.

Mustering all my courage, I asked him to describe the circumstances of his fatal shooting of his common-law wife, Joan Vollner Adams in Mexico City in 1951. I knew this disastrous event was a personal fulcrum for Burroughs, the wound that finally precipitated his art. He had been a blocked writer for years, but at the age of 37, during his trial, he wrote his first book JUNKIE, and QUEER, a book published much later. Burroughs winced and moved out of range of my tape recorder. I practically had to read his lips. It is the only time I ever saw him waver, mumble or appear evasive. It was an enormously uncomfortable moment for both of us.

My book NAKED ANGELS was published in 1976, and I did not see Burroughs again until the Kerouac Conference celebrating the 25th anniversary of ON THE ROAD in Boulder in 1982. Conducting a series of interviews for a docudrama on Kerouac, I ran into Burroughs at the opening of an art show featuring Kerouac's paintings. When I asked him about the paintings, he compared their rough uninformed power to Van Gogh. He was quite drunk that evening, weaving and balanced by a cane that seemed in his hands like a formidable weapon, full of a manic almost diabolic glee that I had only seen when he performed Dr. Benway botching an operation on Saturday Night Live. Later, when I actually did the interview with my film crew, Burroughs kept looking sideways and twitching, a body language that told me he could not wait for it to terminate.

Burroughs was unimpressed by fame and did his best to avoid its consequences. He had written, in NAKED LUNCH, a landmark of postmodernism that had begun as letters to his friend Allen Ginsberg. Writing in Tangiers under the influence of heavy opiates and majoun, a hashish confection, he described the fantasies, debilitations and terrors of addiction from the inside. This was a daring subject matter, but even more important was his startling departure in form. He had written an anti-novel juxtaposing a series of mordantly bizarre burlesque sketches - he called them "routines" - all fragmented, discontinuous, expressing a hallucinated conspiratorial vision with surreal hyperbole. He predicted our catastrophic national appetite for drugs, our unlimited capacity for violence, and the repercussive dangers of police surveillance and state control. He was, in short, an American Orwell.

Stately   photograph by Jon Blumb

THE DEATH OF WILLIAM S. BURROUGHS

by Douglas Brinkley

Queer to think of him now living in Lawrence, Kansas, meticulously dressed in his undertaker suit and gray fedora, a cross between T.S. Eliot and Dashiell Hammett, poking through the cat food at the local Kroger's then out to aim his Smith & Wesson at backyard canvases in the pursuit of instant "shotgun art," winding up reading H.P. Lovecraft by night lamp while in the dry distance the Santa Fe railroad conductor blew his midnight whistle on the lonesome way from Wichita to Topeka. It's so hard to imagine because ever since NAKED LUNCH (first published in Paris) reached the United States - with what NEWSWEEK called "a heavier burden of literary laudations than any piece of fiction since ULYSSES" - its author, William S. Burroughs, had been ordained America's most incendiary artist, a deadpan cubist who used razor-honed words to paint the zeitgeist of post-modernist despair. "Fiction is at least fifteen years behind painting," Burroughs maintained, which explains why his 50-year literary career included both visual and verbal collaborations with the likes of Robert Rauschenberg, David Hockney, George Condo, Philip Taaffe and Keith Haring.

A creator of grim fairy tales for adults, Burroughs spoke to our nightmare fears - and still worse, to our nightmare longings. More than any other postwar wordsmith he bridged generations, in fact, his popularity in the youth culture is greater now than it was during the heady days of the Beats. Over six decades the avant garde grew enchanted with the non-conformity of this Harvard-educated renegade and grandson of the inventor of the Burroughs adding machine, whose family was listed in the St. Louis Social Register. Thus was hatched the myth of a rich kid with pedigree and a Harvard degree who squandered it all away for a syringe of morphine and the life of a Times Square hustler.

In such dream-state works as NAKED LUNCH, THE TICKET THAT EXPLODED and NOVA EXPRESS, Burroughs explored homosexuality, sadism, masochism, authoritarian control, street junkies, greedheads, whorehouse freaks, callous con men, corrupt scientists, Egyp-tologists, money manipulators, and just plain wild boys all with the same brutal, fierce and exact satirical aplomb. At any given time his readers might encounter Mayan codices and Kwakiutl Indians, Billy the Kid and Greta Garbo. "Burroughs has always written for the Space Age," novelist Gary Indiana has noted. "His work addresses readers who want OUT of present slave-planet conditions."

While Larry McMurtry and John Updike often bring characters from one novel to the next, Burroughs recycled phrases, "routines" and person-alities as if they were replacement gears to be snapped into a machine. But there was an almost prophetic nature to some of his notions: back in the 1940s he wrote of "stomach tucks" before liposuction, described a fatal viral epidemic much like AIDS, created a fictional synthetic drug spook-ily similar to crack. Nelson Algren may have written THE MAN WITH THE GOLDEN ARM, but he never actually shot junk: by contrast, NAKED LUNCH is a virtual-reality guide through the highly personal-ized hell of a man who knew the needle firsthand. When Burroughs wrote JUNKIE and NAKED LUNCH in the 1940s and 1950s drugs were not the overwhelming public they are today thanks to the torment of urban crime they've engendered - but as Burroughs maintained long ago, "Drugs are an inevitable part of life." The premonitory knack in his experimental novels enabled Burroughs to identify problems that recur and magnify over time. "Junk is the ideal product," he wrote in NAKED LUNCH, "the ultimate merchandise. No sales necessary. The client will crawl through a sewer and beg to buy.... The junk merchant does not sell his product to the consumer, he sells the consumer to his product. He does not improve and simplify his merchandise. He degrades and simplifies the client."

To Burroughs, "the client" was a consumer society of insatiable addicts, a nation of farmers who claimed no love for the land, just a base lust for more acres. His philosophy was dubbed "The Algebra of Need," the belief that human beings were jaundiced animals on the lowest rung of the great ladder: Wall Streeters who crave money, movie stars who crave fame, politicians who crave power, and junkies who crave a fix. To Burroughs all were equally loathsome; like Mark Twain, he regarded cats as far superior to people. Burroughs never quite joined the modern world order - to him sanity was experimenting with

William's Orgone Box   photograph by Lee Ranaldo

Reich's "Orgone Box" and Korzbski's semantics. "What am I doing here a broken eccentric?" he wrote Jack Kerouac from Tangiers in the early 1950s. "A Bowery evangelist reading books on theosophy in the public library, an old tin trunk full of notes in my coldwater flat...imagining myself a secret world controller, in telepathic contact with Tibetan Adepts."

Politically, Burroughs was a libertarian who believed government should be a tenth its present size. He opposed foreign aid, federal subsidies, censorship, and laws restricting both private sexual conduct between consenting adults and the recreational use of drugs - all, ironically, positions held by William F. Buckley, Jr.. "The word liberal has come to stand for

W.S. Burroughs & Robert Frank, Boulder, 1982   photograph © 1998 Mellon

the most damnable tyranny, a snivelling, mealy-mouthed tyranny of bureaucrats, social workers, psychiatrists, and union officials," Burroughs wrote Kerouac. "The world of 1984 is not even 30 years away."

In this post-Watergate, post-Oliver Stone's "JFK," post-J. Edgar Hoover in drag America, the idea of Big Brother controlling everything has become a commonplace theme, but it was considered science fiction when Burroughs invented the "Nova Mob," a sinister consortium of CIA and bureaucratic gangsters, drug runners, and government power brokers. Burroughs's neo-Boschian world of Mugwumps and Greenboys presaged of today's syndicates and militias, and such archetypal characters as Bradly the Buyer, Hamburger Mary, and Dr. Benway are eerily reminiscent of Michael Milken, Madonna and Dr. Kevorkian. And Burroughs imagined this unlikely pop trinity when fellow Missourian Harry Truman was still President, long before Elvis Presley had recorded a hit single or Brown v. Board of Education integrated our schools.

Burroughs reminded Kerouac of a "Kansas minister with exotic phenomenal fire and mysteries." In ON THE ROAD he profiled Burroughs as "Old Bull" - a man with seven distinct personalities, each worse than the last: "The top personality was an English Lord, the bottom, the idiot. Halfway he was an old Negro who stood in line, waiting with everybody else and said "Some's bastards some's ain't, that's the score." Norman Mailer, however, saw Burroughs more as "a mad prospector up in the mountains who'll shoot you if you come to his cabin at the wrong time." Both were right: he was like a droll Great Plains minister fresh out of a Grant Wood painting, a nasal-twanging millenialist who memorized Spengler, read Celine, dreamed Kafka, dated Ginsberg, befriended Genet, traveled with Kerouac, performed with Bono, and shot guns with Hunter S. Thompson. When punk anarchist Sid Vicious of the SEX PISTOLS sang the Frank Sinatra hit "My Way," it was pure William S. Burroughs. When rocker Patti Smith sneered "Jesus Died For Somebody's Sins But Not Mine," that was pure Burroughs too. Composer Philip Glass was greatly influenced by Burroughs's cut-up methods while singer Tom Waits worked with him on a musical drama. Rock bands such as Insect Trust, Steely Dan, Hüsker Dü, and Throbbing Gristle took their names from NAKED LUNCH (which itself was named by Kerouac). The raucous MTV video hit "Just One Fix" by Ministry used Burroughs as its centerpiece, anointing him the ancient guru of the hard-core underground. Before he committed suicide Nirvana's Kurt Cobain collaborated with Burroughs as well, making the mandatory rock'n'roll pilgrimage to the quiet college town of Lawrence, which William Quantrill had burned and plundered on August 21, 1863.

"Most of the objectives set forth in the 1960s have been realized," Burroughs maintained. "Young people don't seem to realize this when they say to me, 'Do you think the 1960s accomplished anything?' I say 'What!' They don't seem to realize that forty years ago, four-letter words did not appear on printed pages; that when I was in my twenties and thirties, the idea that a Mexican or a black or a queer was anything but a second-class citizen was simply absurd."

It was Burroughs who invented the phrase "heavy metal" in NOVA EXPRESS - and whether or not you like the noise it now describes, there's no overlooking hard rock's impact on youth culture. In fact, it is impossible to understand the Beatles or the Rolling Stones, British Pop Art or Roy Lichtenstein, Francis Bacon or Andy Warhol, John Cage or La Mote Young, the Velvet Underground or Sonic Youth, Sam Shepard or Thomas Pynchon without giving a nod to Burroughs, the first truly postmodern aesthete, a natural born deconstructionist, the elder states-man of the Beat Generation and the granddaddy of punk.

Today every city in America boasts gutter punks - the bored, middle-

photograph by Jon Blumb

class, nihilistic New Age descendants of William S. Burroughs - who read tarot cards, believe trashy science fiction, their pierced and tat-tooed bodies gather into death-rock clubs like "The Twilight Zone." Alienation is a rite of passage, of course, and many gloom-and-doom youths who don't care about saving the rain forests that are already destroyed have found solace in Burroughs' fiction.

The American under-ground long ago baptized Burroughs its high priest of disorientation. "Burroughs is in my opinion...a religious writer," Mailer has noted.

"There is a sense in NAKED LUNCH of the destruction of soul, which is more intense than any I have encountered in any other modern novel." For fifty years, Burroughs has been our authoritative "White Negro," a role he assumed long before Mailer penned his landmark essay or THE NAKED AND THE DEAD was even a pipedream. Astonishingly, it was a role Burroughs played like a straight man to the bitter end. Nobody ever really understood what made him tick; he was beyond the ministrations of Freudian psychiatry or voodoo medicine or the likes of Oral Roberts. Compared with Burroughs Artaud and Breton were naughty cub scouts. Perhaps artist Brion Gysin, who taught Burroughs the cut-up writing technique, came closest stating that "an odd blue light often flashed around under the brim of his hat."

photograph by Jon Blumb

AN INTERVIEW WITH WILLIAM S. BURROUGHS

by John Tytell

This interview was recorded in Burroughs' New York City loft on March 24, 1974.

John Tytell: In 1950 you were studying in Mexico City College. What kind of school was that?

William Burroughs: It was organized for people on the G.I. Bill and classes were in English. I studied archeology, mostly Mexican, and Mayan and Aztec. Aztec is very difficult, Mayan very easy.

JT: Where did you do your undergraduate work?

WB: 1936. Harvard. English lit.

JT: Did you take any courses in modern literature?

WB: Not formally.

JT: Did you read Joyce or Eliot then?

WB: Eliot was there as a visiting professor. I went to one of his lectures, he gave lectures and seminars. Eliot was very much something that people were into at that time.

JT: What modern writers most moved you at that time?

WB: I wasn't really in to modern literature, but Eliot, Joyce, Kafka, Fitzgerald, of course.

JT: They are making a movie of THE GREAT GATSBY.

WB: I'm sure it will be a real mess.

JT: But not at the box office.

WB: I'm not even sure of that. Generally speaking they know what they're doing, but they don't always. They will go all out on these spectaculars that don't work at all. I was just looking the book over myself with the idea of making a film, and there just is no film there - everything's in the prose, you take that away and you've got wooden dialogue and creaky action.

JT: The prose does have an elusive quality so that it appears easy, but underneath the surface is that astonishingly intricate imagery and richness. I think you are right, this will just be a stageshow.

WB: It isn't cinematic.

JT: What did you do after you left Harvard? I'd like to establish a chronology.

WB: A year in Europe studying medicine at the University of Vienna. After that I returned to America and studied psychology briefly at Columbia, then back at Harvard doing graduate work in anthropology. Then a year in New York with an advertising agency. In the army briefly, out again, Chicago where I worked as an exterminator and at various other jobs. Back to New York in 1943. Left in about '46 for Texas, then New Orleans.

JT: When did you leave for Mexico?

WB: 1949. I stayed in Mexico until 1952, South America in 1953, back in New York, in 1953. Then I went to Europe, first to Italy and then Tangiers from about 1954 to 1958. Then Paris. Then between Paris and London during the early sixties. In 1964 I was in Tangiers, in 1965 I was here for a year, and from then on mostly in London.

JT: I would like to ask you specific questions about certain of these years. When you were in New York 1943, where did you live?

WB: Uptown, downtown, all over, around the Village, Columbia.

JT: I heard that you worked as a bartender.

WB: For about three weeks on Bedford Street.

JT: It was at that time you first met Kerouac and Ginsberg. Ann Charters says that Dave Kammerer introduced you. Where had you known Kammerer?

WB: St. Louis: we were brought up together. I'd known him all my life.

JT: I heard that when you first visited Kerouac you were interested in learning how to get seaman's papers?

WB: Vaguely. I did get seaman's papers years later but never used them.

JT: I read in your correspondence that you did what might be termed a "lay analysis" or psychoanalysis of Allen Ginsberg? What was that like?

WB: That's true. It was a very sketchy procedure.

JT: Had you been analyzed?

WB: Oh yes. Waste of time and money.

JT: How did Allen take your analysis?

WB: Well, now he was interested - people like to talk about themselves.

JT: At one time did you share an apartment with Edie Parker, Joan Adams and Kerouac?

WB: Yes. It was a big apartment and I had a room there for about four or five months in '44.

JT: Do you feel that in any way you influenced Kerouac and Ginsberg at that time?

WB: Influenced in what way?

JT: You've written that certain figures leave their impression in terms of speech and language.

WB: Well I should say that Kerouac influenced me much more than I influenced him because I wasn't at all interested in writing at that time, and he was one of several people who told me that I should write. The title of NAKED LUNCH was his, not mine.

JT: Kerouac would later type portions of that novel for you in Tangiers.

WB: That was many years later.

JT: I wanted to ask how that book finally came together, and what role others may have had in helping you assemble it.

WB: One of the key figures was Sinclair Beiles who was working for Girodias at that time. Girodias had seen the novel, not the version that finally appeared but a version that I had before, remember that there were about a thousand pages to this from which the final material was selected, and some of the overflow went into THE SOFT MACHINE, THE TICKET THAT EXPLODED, NOVA EXPRESS and some of it is still unpublished, and in the archives.

JT: Was any of the original material part of QUEER?

WB: No. That was a separate thing and way back.

JT: Carl Solomon told me of reading it and feeling that it wasn't the right time to bring it out.

WB: Ace had no intention of bringing it out. Wyn said I'd be in jail if it was published. But it has very little to do with the subsequent material from which NAKED LUNCH was assembled.

JT: How did you first meet Huncke?

WB: Through Bob Brandenberg who was a sort of marginal hoodlum who used to hang around the West End in 1944.

JT: Huncke told me the story about the morphine syrettes and was it a sawed off shotgun or a pistol?

WB: No, it was a submachine gun.

JT: But that's a fairly large weapon?

WB: This guy stole it and carried it out under his coat.

JT: Was it an army weapon?

WB: Yes. He had smuggled this thing out and nobody wanted to touch it. I finally sort of gave it away to somebody.

JT: Could one get ammunition for that?

WB: Sure, standard 45.

JT: Huncke told me that you maintained an apartment on Henry Street on the lower East Side then.

Aiming .45 Casul Revolver   photograph by Jon Blumb

WB: That's right, I had that apartment for fifteen dollars a month. A walk-in kitchen and a few small rooms.

JT: How did you start with morphine?

WB: Well the syrettes were the beginning. I met this guy named Phil White who bought some of the syrettes from me, and he turned me onto the morphine. Then I started going around with him to doctors.

JT: Getting script, as you call it in JUNKIE. When had opium become illegal?

WB: Since the Harrison Narcotics Act around 1914. But you could still get preparations like paregoric.

JT: Was Huncke a new kind of person for you to have met, or had you met people like him before?

WB: No, I'd not met anyone like Huncke before.

JT: What attracted you to him?

WB: Well, you know, he had some interesting stories. Also, he was associated with Phil White and we would get junk together.

JT: Didn't Huncke introduce you to Bill Garver?

WB: He did. He had been in jail, and then he brought Garver around to Joan's apartment.

JT: Garver was a notorious coat-thief, wasn't he?

WB: That's true. He also had a small income of twenty-five dollars a week from his father which was not enough for his habit. So he had to supplement that by stealing overcoats. When his father died, he came into about three to four hundred dollars a month, that's when he moved to Mexico. Later we lived in the same building. He is Bill Gains in JUNKIE.

JT: Huncke told me that he introduced you to Dr. Kinsey when Kinsey began his research around Times Square.

WB: He did indeed. Kinsey and Ward Pomeroy. We met at a place called The Angler, that was on Eighth avenue between 42nd and 43rd.

JT: Did Kinsey interview you?

WB: No, Pomeroy did.

JT: Did you know Bill Cannastra?

WB: I never met him. I heard a lot about him from Allen Ginsberg, but more particularly from Allen Ansen.

JT: I asked you earlier whether you thought you had in any way influenced Ginsberg or Kerouac, and you said that Kerouac had influenced you more, because he made you aware of writing, but Allen Ginsberg told me that one way that you definitely influenced both of them was with books that you suggested that they read, that he had no introduction to modern literature and that you gave him Hart Crane and Auden and Eliot and other books, Kafka, that you gave Kerouac Spengler.

WB: And perhaps Celine.

JT: Were you reading Wilhelm Reich at the time?

WB: Either then or later.

JT: What about Lucien Carr? Was he part of your circle then?

WB: Yes. I'd known Lucien from St. Louis, introduced to him by David Kammerer. I saw Lucien subsequently in Chicago when I was there.

JT: Did you meet frequently with Kerouac, Ginsberg, Carr, or were your encounters sporadic?

WB: Sporadic. I saw a lot of Dave because I had known him for a long time and he lived right around the corner of Morton Street when I lived in the Village. The others lived uptown, and I saw more of them when I moved there.

JT: When you shared the apartment with Ginsberg, Joan Adams and Edie Parker?

WB: That's right. Edie Parker who married Jack Kerouac.

JT: After Jack had been apprehended as an accessory to Carr's murder of Kammerer?

WB: Not as an accessory but a material witness.

JT: How did that happen? I've heard so many different versions, and that Kammerer had been Carr's scoutmaster.

WB: There was some such connection. Then they took a trip to Mexico, and there was trouble between Kammerer and Lucien's mother.

JT: I read in your correspondence that you and Kerouac wrote a novel based on the friendship and subsequent murder.

WB: We did write such a novel - THE HIPPOES WERE BOILED IN THEIR TANK.

JT: How did you get that title?

WB: It was in a news broadcast about a circus fire, so we used that.

JT: Is the book in your archives?

WB: No, we can't get hold of it. It's with Sterling Lord. Richard Aaron was supposed to come over here to try and recover it.

JT: What led you to leave New York?

WB: Well, there was a definite likelihood of legal difficulties. When I left I went to Texas.

JT: That's when you began farming?

WB: No, it wasn't. I forgot, I first left, and then I came back to New York, and then left again, so it was two times that I left.

JT: Huncke told me that after the New Waverly scene you, Neal Cassady and Huncke returned to New York in a jeep from New Waverly.

WB: That was later.

JT: From reading your letters I could tell that you were hassled by bureaucrats at the time you were farming, or at least that you resented their controls a great deal.

WB: Well, there were cotton allotments and all kinds of rules. We were okay on that, but not always, and then there was a matter of loans that had to be negotiated. It's really no operation for people who are operating with small capital. If anything goes wrong you're wiped out.

JT: So you're totally at the mercy of credit?

WB: Completely.

JT: In the letters you describe that the relativity of the law had never been clearer to you because of your experience with farming. In particular because of the wetbacks, the way they would be encouraged to come in by the state and at the same time there could be penalties, selectively applied.

WB: Very selectively applied. You got in wrong with the authorities and a truck would drive up and take all your wetbacks away, and you'd be left in cotton picking season with no help.

JT: At the same time, any wetback would be earning five times what he could get in Mexico.

WB: But this didn't happen to the big farmers.

JT: Because they had protection?

WB: Yes. In the big ranches the wetbacks were herded all over the place. They had guards with machine guns. They tried to pull a strike once and the guards shot three of them, so they all went back to work. They had no rights.

JT: In New Waverly you also grew grass? Were you farming anything else?

WB: Couldn't farm anything else.

JT: Was the soil bad?

WB: The problem was how were you going to farm, with what? I mean you could get a horse and plow and do subsistence farming.

JT: Cassady and Ginsberg visited you in New Waverly? What was your impression of Cassady?

WB: I thought he was a very pleasant, easy-going person.

JT: I've heard that he was very intense, capable of long monologues.

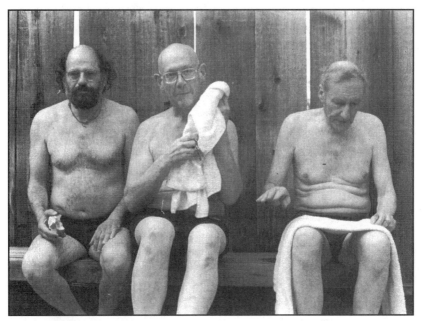

Ginsberg, Whalen & Burroughs at the pool, Boulder, 1976   photograph by Gordon Ball

Was that true then?

WB: I always felt his capacity for silence. I've been with him for eight hours and never exchanged a word.

JT: What kind of driver was he?

WB: Brilliant, a fantastic driver. I had a jeep and the clutch and brakes were out, and he could brake it by putting it into reverse.

JT: I heard that he drove Kesey's bus at high speeds around curves knowing somehow that there was nothing coming the other way.

WB: He was capable of unbelievable feats of instant calculation.

JT: How did you spend your days in New Waverly? Were you writing at that time?

WB: No, no, no. I didn't write anything, hardly, until I was thirty-five. Anyway, I wasn't writing. But there were always things to do, like put a fence around the place, cut wood, walk around.

JT: Was the country beautiful?

WB: It was heavy timber. Oak and persimmon, not too much pine. The kind of country that starts in southern Missouri and goes all the way down to east Texas. There were raccoons and foxes and squirrels and armadilloes.

JT: What led you to invite Huncke to the New Waverly place?

WB: I don't remember.

JT: How long was he there?

WB: Quite a while, four or five months.

JT: Did Kerouac visit you there?

WB: No, he didn't.

JT: He visited you on several other occasions, though?

WB: He lived with me in New Orleans, then later in Mexico.

JT: Had he written THE TOWN AND THE CITY then?

WB: Yes.

JT: Had you seen any of it? Did you know you were a character in it?

WB: I hadn't seen any of it at that time, but he told me I appeared in it.

JT: What was his mood like then?

WB: It was very good.

JT: In one of the letters you mention that on a later visit in Mexico, I think in 1952, he was depressed, uncooperative and unhappy.

WB: He was moody and a little bit paranoid.

JT: Do you think the difficulty he was having getting ON THE ROAD accepted had anything to do with his attitude?

WB: Possibly. But then he seemed to take that rather philosophically. The book was literally years kicking around. Malcolm Cowley liked it, but the editor-in-chief didn't at all, and so there were all those delays which might have been just as well because the timing of the book was good, had it been published earlier, it might not have received the same attention.

JT: That's an interesting point. And he did a lot of writing during the six years between finishing ON THE ROAD and its publication in 1957.

WB: Oh yes. He was always writing.

JT: Can you tell me more about the history of NAKED LUNCH?

WB: I had this great amorphous manuscript. Girodias had seen some of it and had rejected it. I was living in Paris. This was 1958. Allen Ginsberg was also there and he sent selections off to Irving Rosenthal for THE CHICAGO REVIEW, and then THE CHICAGO REVIEW folded in protest after having difficulty with the university over the issue because of my material and something by Kerouac as well, and then Rosenthal published it in BIG TABLE. That was what called it to Girodias' attention. He saw BIG TABLE and said now I want the book. So he sent Sinclair Beiles over to my room who said Girodias wants to publish the book, and he wants it in two weeks. So I got busy, and Brion Gysin helped with typing - Allen had gone - and Sinclair Beiles was most helpful. I was just typing it out and giving it to Beiles with the idea that when we got galley proofs I could decide the final order. But he took one look at it and said leave it the way it is. So it was just really an accidental juxtaposition. And the book was out a month

Coded by Burroughs   photograph by Felver

later.

JT: That's a kind of "automatic" structuring - without any wilfull control. How does that approach Kerouac's ideal of spontaneity?

WB: Kerouac was not thinking of an accidental procedure but of spontaneity in writing. He was always very opposed to writing with "cut-ups" which is, in a sense, an accidental procedure. Kerouac believed the first version was the best, and I have never found this to be true. I work over things and edit them very carefully.

JT: When Girodias took NAKED LUNCH you were living at the "Beat Hotel," 9 rue Git le Couer?

WB: And Olympia Press was around the corner. Girodias had inherited the press from his father, it was then called The Dial Press, and they had originally come from Manchester. Girodias' brother later translated NAKED LUNCH into French, and Gallimard took it a year after it had been published in English.

JT: Wasn't there an obscenity trial in the States?

WB: Two, the first was in Boston where we won on appeal, then in Los Angeles we won in the lower courts. By that time it was pretty well established that there was no censorship on the written word.

JT: Has Henry Miller been a writer who in any way influenced you?

WB: No.

JT: Had you read de Sade?

WB: I looked at de Sade when I was in Paris. Girodias had some translations, but I found it heavy going.

JT: Did you have any interest in Gertrude Stein when you were at Harvard?

WB: I read THREE LIVES there.

JT: Later, did Brion Gysin try to interest you in her work?

WB: No, but he knew her. She was the one who told Paul Bowles that he shouldn't stay in Paris but should find some other place.

JT: What were your lodgings like at 9 Rue Git le Couer?

WB: A single room. I had an alcohol stove in the room. There was no phone, but I had red tile floors. It was very cheap.

JT: Judging from the letters, Ginsberg, Kerouac, everyone seems to have stayed there.

WB: At different times.

JT: Where was the Villa Delirium?

WB: That was the Muniria in Tangiers where I lived for a number of years.

JT: I read in your letters that when you first went to Tangiers you lived in a whorehouse. What was that like? Faulkner once said in an interview that a whorehouse was the ideal place for a writer to live.

WB: It was not that kind of a whorehouse at all. It was just a small place where Tony Dutch who ran it rented out rooms. Tony was a great cook and if you wanted to take meals there you could. After that I moved into the Muniria where I stayed off and on for many years. It's changed hands many times. First it was owned by a Belgian whose son was involved with smuggling, then it was run by an ex-madam from Indochina. She had an "in" with the authorities and ran it for many years without trouble. She sold out and a retired British civil servant took it over.

JT: I have some other miscellaneous questions. What about the story that your first wife was a Hungarian countess?

WB: She wasn't. Her name was Ilse Herzfeld Klapper, they were solid, wealthy bourgeois Jewish people in Hamburg. She had to get out because of Hitler and went to Yugoslavia, and I married her in Athens to get her into the States. She supported herself by working in a travel agency and various jobs. She was very efficient. She was secretary for Ernst Toller, a leftist playwright who tried to commit suicide several times. But he always arranged it so that someone would come and prevent him. And she was a very punctual person. If she went to lunch at twelve she would be back at twelve-thirty. It just so happened that she ran into an old acquaintance in the street and was ten minutes late, and when she returned he was dead in the bathroom. At his funeral she met Kurt Kaszner, a famous Austrian actor who had married a very rich American girl. She became his secretary. Then Mrs. Kaszner died, and the servants said he had poisoned her and she was dug up again, but there was nothing in it, she died of natural causes. Then she worked for John le Touche as his secretary until he died under mysterious circumstances.

JT: I've heard that you had applied to the O.S.S. during the war?

WB: I did and was not accepted. I went down and saw Bill Donovan with a letter of introduction from an uncle, but he referred me to somebody else and nothing happened.

JT: You mentioned that you were in the army?

WB: For a short time, five months. I was stationed in St. Louis.

JT: When was that?

WB: During the war, in 1942, I think.

JT: Do you record your dreams?

WB: I write them down.

JT: How do you do it?

WB: I wake up six times in the course of the average night. I'll just make a few notes. If it's of interest, I transcribe it in the morning. I get at least half, perhaps more, of my material from dreams, characters, sets,

William, Peter & Gregory   photograph by Felver

etc.

JT: Can you tell me about the Dutch Schultz filmscript?

WB: I had been interested in Dutch Schultz for a long time, having read his famous last words. There were about 2,000 of them since he was shot on October 23rd at 10PM and he died about 24 hours later, and they had a police stenographer at his bedside. Anyway, he presumably wrote all his words down, though he was delirious and the stenographer may have missed words. Then David Budd came over with quite a bit of research material, that is to say, a series of articles that had appeared in COLLIERS by his lawyer, Dixie Davis. I became interested and wrote a film treatment which was about fifteen pages, this was published in HARPER'S. Then someone named Harrison Starr wanted to produce this as a movie so he paid a sum of money - ten thousand dollars or something like that - for me to write a film play which I wrote, and that was published by Grollier Press as THE LAST WORDS OF DUTCH SCHULTZ. There were other negotiations and I went on to write a full length film script, a shooting script in 1971.

JT: Wasn't part of NAKED LUNCH written like that, as a film script?

WB: No, in play form, but I'm talking about a shooting script, like indoors, medium shot, or close-up. So that was 195 pages. Richard Seaver is publishing that with a lot of stills. But the film was never made.

JT: How come?

WB: Well, the people were interested, but it was expensive, all gangster films are expensive to make.

JT: Is anyone trying to film NAKED LUNCH?

WB: Brion Gysin did a script, but it seems to be up in the air.

JT: Years ago you said you were writing a Zen western novel about a gunfighter.

WB: I never actually wrote it.

JT: Can you tell me about Kells Elvins?

WB: I met him at the age of twelve at the John Burroughs school. He was at Harvard in 1938 when we wrote the story called "Twilights Last Gleaming" which was published almost verbatim in NOVA EXPRESS. That story was the beginning of Dr. Benway.

19

JT: What was the John Burroughs school?

WB: Just a private day school in Clayton, Missouri. We moved out to Clayton which was a suburb of St. Louis, the school was right down the road and Kells lived up the road.

JT: So you knew him since childhood.

WB: And I wrote to him in 1961 saying that the story would appear in NOVA EXPRESS which does mention that he is the co-author, and found out from his mother that he had died about four months before that.

JT: In your last books you seem to be using cut-ups more selectively than previously.

WB: I use them very selectively now. You see, MINUTES TO GO was experimental, now I may make a cut-up of a page and only use a sentence or two.

JT: They seem to be more deliberately used in THE WILD BOYS, and the result is greater impact jarring you into a dream or different reality.

WB: Just cut up something, and suddenly you'll get a sentence that's right. Like the technology of writing that I'm going into in this course. This sentence came out of a cut-up; "Technology requires a why." You have to know what you're doing to figure everything out while you're doing it.

JT: That's an odd word choice, technology rather than technique.

WB: But it's the same thing, technology or technique, it's a way of doing something.

JT: How do you find teaching at CCNY? Have you taught before?

WB: I just gave two lectures at the University of the New World in Switzerland in 1972, I think. I do enjoy teaching at CCNY, I don't know whether my pupils are learning anything, but I'm learning a great deal, and making my own ideas explicit. I'm considering the question of whether there is a technology for writing as there is for learning how to fly, or for learning physics, or engineering. Now how many of those who fly have taken courses in flying, or how many physicists have taken courses in physics - well, obviously all of them - but how many writers have taken courses in writing?

JT: You never took courses in writing.

WB: More haven't than have.

JT: One wonders whether it is a craft that can be taught - I can see how you can be helped by a critic sensitive to your own strengths and weaknesses.

WB: Well, following it right through, take learning to fly or physics, you're wasting your time unless you meet certain qualifications. If you're going to be a flier you've got to have coordination, a certain degree of intelligence, or you're wasting your time. Given that, these things can be taught. But given all the qualifications for writing, whatever those may be, like some ability to empathize with other people's minds - well a writer like Beckett doesn't need that because he's on his own, going inside, so it may not always apply. Another factor may be the physical discipline, spending long hours writing. For example, if you are learning something like skiing or karate, you have to have an instructor, and if you do it and don't do it right your performance is going to decline this is not true of writing. Writing is learned by writing. Kerouac, when I first met him, had already written a million words, and that was when he was twenty-three. And lots of it was very bad.

JT: There was this early novel called THE SEA IS MY BROTHER.

WB: He had many different manuscripts, and I read most of it, and

21

thought it was pretty bad. But writers learn from bad writing, but a skier does not learn from bad skiing.

JT: There is a more direct relationship between experience and practical act with writing than most of us imagine. I guess good writers reach a point when they can finally do it, as with Kerouac, when he could become, as it were, spontaneous.

WB: At any rate I've learned about writing and the technology of writing by teaching this course.

JT: Do you plan to write about that?

WB: I'm having all the lectures transcribed. Naturally I have extensive notes, but there's always extemporizing, questions.

JT: Do you have good students?

WB: They are quite a receptive group.

JT: I wanted to tell you that a number of my students seem to be sexually excited by a book like THE WILD BOYS, especially by the association of violence and sexuality, even in NAKED LUNCH they admit to being turned on despite the elements of comedy or parody.

WB: I find that sexual passages are the most difficult to write. I don't mean the pornographic novels, the ones Girodias was publishing, because they're not sexy at all. They're very easy to write. People write them as fast as they can type. That pornographic style derives from FANNY HILL, which is about as unsexy as you can get. Actually, most of those books are written by junkies, and they have no sexual feeling for what they are writing.

JT: There are sections of your work that play with pornographic situations very successfully, like "Seeing Red" in THE WILD BOYS where a man comes through customs with a dirty picture that is left undescribed but which causes paroxysms for the officials.

WB: I think description of any sort is difficult, but sexual passages have to be written and rewritten.

JT: Does this have to do with a basic repression we all have, a fear to describe sex?

WB: No, it's just as hard to describe anything. Straight narrative is easy. If I attend to a narrative I can write it almost as fast as I can type.

JT: There seems to be a return to narrative elements in your recent books, THE WILD BOYS and EXTERMINATOR! You seem to be using experimental devices more sparingly.

WB: With more deliberate intent, I think.

photograph by Felver

JT: Could you define obscenity in literature?

WB: I don't think it means anything. What they mean is explicit sex scenes, but that's all soft-core now, there's virtually no censorship left on the written word. Where it might occur is if you have something out of the hard-core circuit. There has been some trouble with "Last Tango."

JT: If that's true, will shame and fear be less an agency of control in this society?

WB: Undoubtedly. But of course it is confined to certain areas. I think a very healthy degree of liberation has occurred. You read the Presidential Report in which they said that 50% of people who saw sex on film found that they were sexually freer. Just the impact of seeing people doing these things on the screen makes people realize "Well, why in the hell should anyone worry about it?" If the actor is willing to get up there without any mask on, how can you be ashamed of it?

JT: Michael McClure once wrote that his intention was "to free the word fuck from its chains." Has that happened?

WB: It has: there are no chains there.

JT: And no future possibility of chains?

WB: I doubt it, unless something drastic happens.

JT: You seem, more than most writers, to have been occupied with kinds of scientific inquiry, and this is reflected in your story situations, for example the character in THE WILD BOYS who stores electricity during shock therapy and then releases it through his eyes as a death ray. At the same time, I don't feel that you can be seen as a science fiction writer.

WB: I've talked to a lot of science fiction writers about this. The younger and more progressive ones maintain that the old categories are breaking down, and science fact has overtaken science fiction. In books like THE TERMINAL MAN the subject is not what's going to happen in three hundred years, but things that can and have been done right now. So the ideas about science fictions are changing as science overtakes it.

JT: Do you read science fiction?

WB: When I have time, but only when I can find any that's good. I'll get a stack and most of it is terrible though there are some good ideas, but there are very few that can convince you that it ever could have happened anywhere.

JT: Have you read anything by Rudolph Wurlitzer?

WB: I read NOG and liked it.

JT: What about someone like Robbe-Grillet?

WB: Haven't read him. I saw an excellent movie based on his work.

JT: What about Beckett?

WB: Well, yes. I would think of Beckett in the same way as Genet, as a writer that I admire very much. I've read practically everything Genet has written. He's a very great writer and not writing anymore.

JT: You met him in Chicago, didn't you, in 1968?

WB: Genet said there were two things: me and the French language, I've put one into the other et c'est faites. With Beckett I like the early novels best, like WATT and MALONE DIES. Now he's getting too hermetic.

JT: Rather than simply informing us of a vision of the future, as in THE WILD BOYS, I feel the ultimate end of your fiction is a kind of alchemy - magic based on precise and incantatory arrangement of language to create particular effects, such as the violation of Western conditioning.

WB: I would say that that was accurate, but I would also say that I am creating a character. And my characters are often a composite: say I have a dream of a character who looks like this, then I'll find a picture or a person, and then maybe a character in someone's else's story. One tries to create a vision of a living being. Of course the beginning of writing, and perhaps of all art, was related to the magical. Cave painting, which is the beginning of writing - after all, remember that the written word is an image we forget this but we don't have a pictorial writing but the written word is an image and painting and writing were originally one and the same. The purpose of those paintings was magical, that is to produce the effect that is depicted.

JT: Is your intention shamanistic, to ward off disaster?

WB: Not necessarily disaster, but certainly to produce effects. For example, all primitive sculpture is magical, but as soon as these things are sold to tourists, they have no vitality. The saying is that painting, writing and sculpture are traditionally magic, and that it is intended to produce certain effects.

JT: Like the sense of transformation implicit in the rate of change in all of your writing?

WB: There is also the question of the actual relations between formal ritual magic and writing. People who are into ritual magic like Aleister Crowley - he may have been a competent black magician but he is not a good writer, in fact he's not readable.

JT: Have you studied magic formally or involved yourself in any kind of cult systems?

WB: Well, the whole content of the Mayan books is obviously magical, but we can't understand very much of it because Bishop Landa burned so much of the writing.

JT: Have you studied any other non-Western procedural maps like THE BOOK OF THE DEAD? Or gnostic texts like the CABALA?

WB: Not very deeply. I've looked at THE BOOK OF THE DEAD. I've read a lot of the literature of magic, but never involved myself very deeply.

JT: Is there any practical accommodation of magic in your work as a writer?

WB: Well, I simply feel that all magic is magic. That is if you get a very subtle evocation of the 1920s in Fitzgerald...

JT: Yes. But that's "magic" in a romantic sense, the idea of evoking a memory onto a page and while that's beautiful, I was thinking of weaving a spell.

WB: But "weaving a spell" is magic. Now you've got the kind of magic that newspapers are involved in, people like Luce who were quite consciously capable of creating events. There is a very definite technique for doing that, and some of it is very much like magic - they stick someone full of pins and then show the picture to millions of people and they will get an effect. Do you realize to what extent being on the front cover of TIME is a kiss of death? The Nobel Prize is another one. Hearst used to say that he didn't write the news, he made it. But that is all negative magic which

W.S. Burroughs at Steven Lowe's House   photograph by Allen Ginsberg

EINSTEIN'S BRAIN IS PICKLED IN KANSAS

A Discussion of Film with William S. Buroughs & Friends

by Neil Hennessy

NEIL HENNESSY: What was the last movie you went to see?

WILLIAM S. BURROUGHS: I'm trying to wonder, I'm trying to figure

NH: I think James said the last movie he thinks you saw was Outbreak.

WSB: Yes, it was Outbreak, yes it was called Outbreak, but I was very confused about where it was taking place; whether the general was sitting right in the town where it was about to blow up or not.

NH: I thought that was interesting. The theme was the virus outbreak which has been a favourite of yours for a while, and there's actually been a rash of those types of movies that have come out, I thought that was a nice tip of the hat. You've said you're not an avid film-goer, but you've had a lot of acting jobs in the last ten years.

WSB: Well, small ones, yes, though I'm not much of an actor, no not at all.

NH: I was wondering how your interest in film was affected by your work with Antony Balch?

WSB: We did film experiments, Towers Open Fire, The Cut-Ups, Bill and Tony. You see, they stopped experimenting with their medium., although they did some in the early days - you know running backwards and speeding up that kind of thing - but they very soon dropped that whole experimental approach.

NH: This is a question that's related to the early days of film. There's a specific passage in The Last Words of Dutch Schultz that I was wondering about. It was in the "ACTION" half of the text: "Sex scene projected... the boy's red back and buttocks on red brick houses... nipples, rose wallpaper, red hair on red jars in drugstore window." Although I know that sexual imagery isn't at all foreign to your work, the juxtaposition and fading of a sexual image to a mundane worldly image is something that Luis Bunuel and Dali did a lot of.

WSB: Yes.

NH: I was wondering if you were familiar with their work.

WSB: Which ones?

NH: Un Chien Andalou and L'Age D'Or.

WSB: Sure, both.

NH: Had you seen them in Paris? Were they around in those days?

WSB: I don't know when I saw them, but I've seen them several times. Luis Bunuel, he was the one that died in Mexico City not too long ago wasn't he?

NH: Yes, I think so.

WSB: At the age of eighty-three they learned that he was gay [laughs].

NH: You wrote Dutch Schultz in columns, separating the action from the dialogue, which immediately put me in mind of some of your columns pieces.

WSB: Oh yes, sure.

NH: In this case the intersection points occur on almost every line, and it's a lot less subtle. Did having to separate the story so distinctly into dialogue and action cause any difficulties in writing?

WSB: What?

NH: Did having to split the action from the words cause any problems in writing it?

WSB: No, not as such, no.

NH: After Dutch Schultz in The Wild Boys and Port of Saints you continue to write with camera directions like "zoom in", "close-up", "flashback", "on screen", "cut back to". It reminded me of something that Michael Ondaatje said after he wrote The Collected Works of Billy the Kid, he said, "I was writing the book no-one would pay me to film." Different from Ondaatje I figured that you were writing the book that no-one could film.

WSB: Well, yes, when I first started that I really had very little knowledge of film and what is entailed. For example my Last Words of Dutch Schultz would have taken God knows how many hours. There are definite rules you see. There aren't very definite rules for writing, I can't tell anyone how to write, but you can tell somebody how to write a film script. There was a very good book, what's it called? He said there must be a crucial change after about ten minutes in the film. He was using as his model Chinatown, which I saw. I don't remember just when that ten minutes occurred, but ten minutes into the film there's got to be a shift, there has to be a crucial change.

NH: And that's just in order to keep the audience's interest, or is that from an artistic standpoint?

WSB: Oh no, no, it's more to keep the audience interested I guess. There are definite as I said there are these definite rules about film scripts. If they don't stick to these rules they don't work as a film. As I said he used Chinatown for his model. What was the name of that book? It was a very good book, it's called uhhh, maybe James would know. Hey, what's going on in there? Oh maybe James is washing.... [He gets up to go find James who comes back and informs me that the book is Screenplay: The Foundations of Screenwriting, by Sid Field].

NH: Blade Runner: A Movie, was that ever intended to be a film?

WSB: No, not really.

NH: Though the title is Blade Runner: A Movie there seems to be much less camera instructions, you stick to more of a straight narrative style. Was it because you might have felt constricted in The Wild Boys by having to always relate what the camera is doing, what the camera's eye is seeing?

WSB: What do you mean?

NH: There are no camera directions, whereas in The Wild Boys there would be things like...

WSB: Oh yeah...

NH: Things like "close up on this person", and then you move on to something else, whereas in Blade Runner you just stick to the action.

WSB: Yes, it seemed more compatible with film. I'm not interested in film writing at this point.

JAMES GRAUERHOLZ: Neil, this is Wayne Propst.

WAYNE PROPST: Hi Neil.

JG: Since you're trying to tape and we're all chattering and carrying on, if you wouldn't mind doing that part of the afternoon for a few minutes with Neil in your bedroom you'll have more concentration and the tape will come out better.

WSB: All right. [Move to Burroughs's bedroom.]

NH: Film and film metaphors are almost ignored in Cities of the Red Night, but it becomes important again in The Place of Dead Roads, it's almost a controlling metaphor with the Director, and then Kim trying to shoot holes through the master film. He's trying to get all the Johnsons into space, whereas in The Western Lands all of a sudden the role of the Director changes when you introduce the Egyptian mythology,

Painterly   photograph by Jon Blumb

and it becomes an individual thing. I was wondering how you reconciled the Egyptian mythology with your own.

WSB: Well you don't need to. You don't need to reconcile it. It's a viable mythology in that it explains... [David Ohle enters with plate of crackers, cheese, and smoked fish] Good, good. Oh great thank-you, you gotta pass that.

DAVID OHLE: A smoked fish.

WSB: Yes, a smoked fish. Well the thing is that..

WP: Hey, Jim....

WSB: Help yourself.

NH: Thank-you.

WSB: The preservation of the physical body is not the way to go for immortality. In other words, you don't get out of the body by going deeper into it. The seven souls were, in many cases, in irreconcilable conflict: that's what we know as neuroses. First we have the Secret Name, the Director, then we have the Technician, then the Ba, the heart.

WP: Want another drink?

WSB: Yes.

WP: Can I get you something?

NH: Yes, I'll have the same.

WP: The same as Bill?

NH: Yes.

WSB: The Ba, then the Ka, which was the double, which was the guide into the Land of the Dead. The interests of the Ba were similar, were synonymous with the interests of the person. Then there was memory, and then the physical body. You can see that the first four, oh there was the Guardian Angel I forgot, the first four of the seven were immortal and not in danger. They went back for another film you see, whereas the other three had to take their chances in The Land of the Dead. You see their interests were not at all compatible. What we call neuroses being precisely the expression of this incompatibility of interest, irreconcilable conflict of interest.

WP: Here, this will be yours, and this will be yours [hands a drink to Burroughs, and one to me]. Yours is slightly larger than his, OK great. Your glass for future reference is slightly larger than Bills.

NH: OK. It seems that whereas before Kim was fighting for all the Johnsons, it becomes this personal battle, the same with Joe the Dead.

WSB: He's fighting for all the Johnson's because their interests are compatible. The creed, it was just the compatibility of interest. In other words I feel that I would fight for a system which is something that I myself would want, otherwise it's nonsense.

NH: Moving on to dreams, do you see any relationship between dreams and film? I often see film references and film words creep into your work when you're dealing with dreams, especially My Education: A Book of Dreams.

WSB: Well I'll tell you, Hollywood's idea of dreams is slow-motion. Everything starts moving in s l o o o w motion and you know it's a dream. Hollywood doesn't do well when they deal with dreams.

WP: Dreams are often a step down from what was already a bad movie.

WSB: It goes further, even less, even worse! [Laughter] I didn't see the, did you see The Great Gatsby?

WP: Yeah.

WSB: I would like to see it. At times it really carries you back with the tunes I suppose.

WP: Well, what happened is they got carried away with glitz; they spent all their dust on sets and old cars and elegant clothes, and about ten cents on dialogue. It suffered, it was a spectacular look at that era physically, that was the really neat part of it.

WSB in boat   photograph by Allen Ginsberg

WSB: How about the tunes? Do you remember any tunes, any songs?

WP: Oh, no.

WSB: Those really, those were the real expressions I was listening to in 1927.

WP: James could probably recall the music better than I.

WSB: Old music: Melancholy Baby, Angry Angry, [singing] "Angry only for you". Angry and Don't Be Like That, and old Dead Man Blues, of course, by Jelly Roll Morton.

WP: They ought to make a movie of that, what was the name of it? It was simply called Fitzgerald, that autobiography, not autobiography, but biography you gave me of Fitzgerald.

WSB: Sure.

WP: That reads in many ways as a more interesting story than Great Gatsby, his life itself and his wacky wife and all the other strange things.

WSB: Oh yeah, Zelda.

WP: Zelda.

WSB: Zelda, she died in a fire in the sanitarium where she was confined.

NH: I thought a lot of the problem with The Great Gatsby was that the more powerful scenes just couldn't be captured on film.

WSB: You will find in some cases that visual passages cannot be translated into film, like the end of The Great Gatsby you know, you can't do it. You can do the images but it wouldn't fit; or The Dead by Joyce, how are you going to put that into film?

DO: They've got a film of it.

WSB: I know they have.

DO: What's his name...

WSB: I know they have.

DO: John Huston, I've never seen it.

WSB: But there are cases where they cannot, where only words will do it, as they can't do it in film, in film alone - maybe with help but I doubt they could. There are other cases where one image is worth ten pages of description. They're not the same medium. Words evoke, and images sometimes do, and they sometimes don't. Well, yes I've heard

Signing   photograph by Felver

about the film, have you seen it?

NH: No, I haven't.

WSB: I haven't either.

DO: I heard it was very good.

WSB: I guess so, I guess so.. Why don't you bring a chair?

DO: No, I'm just temporarily here.

WSB: There are cases where the image really does it, and cases where it
doesn't, it just blurs it.

NH: I've often thought that the movies they made of Hemingway's
books are just atrocious.

WSB: Oh my God! The Snows of Kilimanjaro. Here is one of the best stories about death in the English language and they pin a happy ending on it. The plane comes flying in with penicillin which wasn't even invented at that time, you see that story starts in 1927. There wasn't any penicillin or any antibiotics. If they had got there any sooner it wouldn't have done much good for an infection that advanced, you know for a major infection they had nothing. Even now it would be very difficult to save someone with that advanced, massive an infection. That was just terrible. That was the worst, what was the other?

WP: Farewell to Arms, oh my God! [laughter]

WSB: The ending of the book was, "I tried saying good-bye to her but it was like saying good-bye to a statue. I left the hospital and walked home in the rain." That's a perfect ending, you see him walking home in the rain, but oh no, in the film he picks her up in his arms, the bells are all ringing all over the city, and he's saying, "Peace! Peace!" [Laughter] Oh my God!

NH: The other thing, probably my favourite passage in the book was when, and this is long before The Old Man and the Sea, where Hemingway almost lets one of his characters wax metaphorical and he starts talking about ants in the fire, but of course he just dismisses it. That's something that just can't be carried into film.

WSB: Yes. I saw A Farewell to Arms but I don't think I saw The Old Man and The Sea, I didn't feel like I was up to it really, and then there was...

DO: Spencer Tracy.

WSB: Yes, that's right.

DO: The old man with a kind of a swarthy make-up job on him.

WSB: He was getting pretty old.

WP: The first time I saw it I was a young teenager and I couldn't wait to get out of the theatre. Oh it was bad.

DO: You would have missed the only interesting scene of all when they brought the dead fish up on shore.

WP: Right, no I did see that. When you're a kid that made it worth going to, but it was just something that when you're a kid was incredibly tedious.

DO: It really was disappointing.

WP: Later when I saw it in college it was better.

DO: We have another fish in there so don't hold back.

WSB: Well, it's not that, my hands are all greasy. Help yourself, dig right in.

NH: Thanks.

WSB: Yes, I was disappointed in all the films they made of his books. They're not the same medium. Did you see The Treasure of the Sierra Madre?

NH: No, I haven't.

WSB: That was a great film, and I read the book, and it just didn't compare with the film. The film was very good, and that is a truism: most good films are based on mediocre books. The Treasure of the Sierra Madre , the novel version, is not much. That Humphrey Bogart was very good, did a great job, he stole the show.

NH: In My Education you often use film words, like "On set", "Scene shifts", "On stage". Do your dreams have a cinematic quality?

WSB: Yes, well, they are similar to film in that they have sets, characters, and dialogue. I was never that interested in film because I never had a sense for film equipment.

NH: When you said that good films are often based on mediocre books I thought about Naked Lunch. I certainly wouldn't call that a mediocre book, and I thought the film adaptation was excellent, however it's probably because he didn't even try...

WSB: He didn't even try to film it. No, thank God. When David [Cronenberg] called I said, "I hope you don't expect me to write the script". He said, "No, not at all." I thought, "That's great".

NH: It makes your job easier.

WSB: Yup, it makes my job a lot easier. I didn't feel it was a book that was particularly adaptable to film because there's so much talk involved. But I think he did a good job because it turned out to be a Cronenberg film. Naturally, well that's fine, that's the way it should be. Have you

Reading 1992   photograph by Jon Blumb

ever seen the, no you wouldn't necessarily, have you been to Tangiers?

NH: No.

WSB: No, well here's a guy sitting here, and somebody sitting here, now the backdrop behind them, the backdrop was Central Park.

NH: Really? I thought it was all filmed in Toronto.

WSB: It was. It was, but there are plenty of backdrops of Central Park. It was going to be filmed in Tangiers; they came over and they were going to do a lot of filming there. Then the Gulf War came up and they decided, and I think wisely, not to do it. So they bought all that stuff, from Tangiers, that whole street, the ironworks the forgers and everything else, they bought it, and brought it back to Canada. They bought that cat in Tangiers as well.

NH: That's interesting. In My Education there was even a dream where you say, "This is a film," and someone says, "Get off the stage." It seemed that this time film wasn't really acting as a metaphor, but as a structure whereby it's easier to convey your dreams. One of the characteristics of film is that you can move from image to image and it doesn't have anything to do with their proximity, notions of feeling connect things.

WSB: Well that is the specialty of film; that is, film can direct your attention towards a curtain or a rod or something like that, and a play can't do that. In film you can show a picture of a dagger that will be used later. In other words you can direct people's attention to things that will later become important.

NH: Yes. Here's a quotation from My Education: "How are shifts made in a dream? How does one get say, from one room to another? By shifting the context you are in."

WSB: That's part of it yes. The context like poker dice a very complicated poker dice. In my dream last night was some woman I'd never seen before, and I hope I never see her again. She came through the door in the house where I used to live in St. Louis, outside of St. Louis on Price Road. At the same time it was a number of overlays of places and houses where I had been. Some that I can't recall at all.

NH: And yet when you're in a dream you can change those things so quickly that you almost have the eye of a camera, especially in the flying dreams - something that you'd never be able to do. Your perspective can go anywhere.

WSB: Of course. There are no rules in dreams.

NH: Anyhow just to sort of close this so I can get this [tape recorder] out of your face and we can move on to some more interesting things, my sort of basic idea that I've been leading up is that film has the same immediacy of dreams so that it is a virtual history in the dream mode...

WSB: Yes.

NH: By using dreams and film metaphors extensively in your writing you seem to be giving us a substantial body of work that is literature in the filmic mode.

WSB: I don't know quite what you're talking about. It doesn't make much sense to me.

NH: By using the techniques...

WSB: Well...

NH: Oh sorry.

WSB: Sure. There are techniques in film which are at times similar to dreams, but as I said Hollywood is not at its best when it deals with dream material.

NH: Getting back to something you said way earlier about the ten minute rule, have you ever seen Sympathy for the Devil?

WSB: I don't think so no.

NH: Godard's movie? That violates that ten minute rule and it just becomes monotony. Out of an hour and a half film about 45 minutes to an hour of it is just The Rolling Stones dicking around in the studio recording Sympathy for the Devil.

WSB: No I saw, no it wasn't Sympathy for the Devil it was something else with Mick Jagger. It was about Hassan I Sabbah and the Assassins and so on. What was the name of that? It wasn't Sympathy for the Devil was it Gimme Shelter? I don't know. [The movie Burroughs refers to is Nick Roeg's Performance (Warner Bros. 1970) in which Mick Jagger discusses HIS and the Assassins]

WP: You know what I thought you meant when you said "Ten Minute Rule"? The Ten Minute Rule here in Lawrence was a law that was passed right after Quantrill attacked the town, burnt it to the ground, and killed all the adult males.

WSB: Did he get..?

WP: Fifteen. But that's the rule that any group of riders consisting of more than three men had to wait for ten minutes on the edge of town before they could come into town.

NH: That's interesting.

WSB: Well you know why Quantrill was so remarkably successul? The mayor of the town for some reason impounded all the guns.

WP: Yup.

WSB: That was so stupid, I mean you know...

WP: I remember why.

WSB: Why?

WP: He thought - and he was right - there were infiltrators that were spies in the community and in his efforts to disarm the spies...

WSB: He disarmed the town.

WP: Probably, as with gun control it's the same today, the spies all kept their guns and the good citizens turned theirs in.

WSB: The stupidest thing is that the pro-gun people never brought out the Quantrill story because they know that if they had been ready for him as they should have been they would have cut him to pieces. They should have set up five or six expert marksmen to get Quantrill. That's the best way to ambush any invaders.

WP: Some of these older buildings around town have viewing areas on the very top floor, they're look-out stations.

WSB: Well sure.

WP: Some people think that those were after Quantrill, those were before Quantrill in many cases, and what they really were for was not observation to speak of, they were sniper posts. That's what they really were for.

NH: Do you ever try to control your dreams?

WSB: Oh well ahh, to some extent. Yes of course we all do, as we try to control any of our circumstances. Oh yes, you've read the Don Juan books haven't you?

NH: Yes.

WSB: Well he says to see your hands in dreams is very important. I've had some interesting experiences seeing my hands in dreams. One time I looked in the mirror and my face was not black, it was mulatto - an elder person in any case - but a definite person; I would recognise him if I ever saw him. I looked down at my hands and they were still white. Now here I am in the washroom looking at the mirror; why I am a Negro but my hands are white is not clear. It's something I do not

Wicked brass bear claws at Burroughs' house   photograph by Lee Ranaldo

understand... Someone here has Einstein's brain. A few blocks from here is Einstein's brain.

DO: That's right.

WSB: Oh magnificent!

NH: I guess that brings it to a close.

JG: I would guess that's probably a great facility.

WSB: Yeah, anyway, anyway a film maker went to see the doctor, went to see the man. So he's looking around, a very old man and you never see what he's sort of looking at. Anyway he says, "What are you going to do with a piece of Einstein's brain?" Well he says, "Not much, there's probably not much use left in it. Any possibility of learning anything from it is gone, it's been dead for so long", so he asked him, "Do you want to know the secrets of the universe?" and he said, "Yes, yes." I would have told him, "If you knew the secrets of the universe they'd either drive you crazy or you wouldn't understand them at all." But I can't understand the why. I would never, I don't want to know the secrets of the universe at all. Only the secrets that are relevant to my immediate presence and purpose.

NH: Like at the end of My Education, you're just "scratching the surface".

WSB: Yes, of course.

Kerouac Conference, Boulder 1992   photograph copyright © 1998 Mellon

A CONVERSATION WITH ALLEN GINSBERG

by John Tytell

Int: What was Burrough's impact on you and Kerouac in the mid-forties?

Ginsberg: Kerouac and I went to see Burroughs in his apartment around Riverside Drive below Columbia, Ninety-second Street. We were curious. We understood that Burroughs was very intelligent and to us mysterious because he had been to Europe in the thirties, and had married a Hungarian countess, we thought, to get her out of Europe. He showed us pictures he had of Berlin friends in 1936, and told us about people going around and saying, "Won't you have some uppies, my dear?" for cocaine, introducing that whole mythology of old bohemian European use of drugs.

Int: Had you tried drugs before meeting Burroughs?

Ginsberg: No.

Int: So that was a crucial introduction?

49

Ginsberg: He didn't immediately introduce drugs at all. It wasn't until about a year later through Huncke and Vicky Arminger who was in that auto crash with me.

Int: The one that Jane Kramer describes?

Carl Solomon: Before you went to P.I.? [Columbia Psychiatric Institute]

Ginsberg: There were a lot of Benzedrine inhalers so the first drug was speed which was introduced by Vicky rather than Bill, and then around '45 or '46 through Huncke and Bill Garver and Phil White there was morphine on the scene. So I took morphine at about the same time Bill first did, in the same week. He has described that situation, meeting Huncke, and trying to unload some morphine not knowing really what it was. Bill had a gun he was trying to get rid of, and so he traded it for a box of stolen Syrettes of morphine - these were war stocks of morphine that soldiers carried around as part of their first aid. Grass didn't come in until about a year later, in '47.

Int: Was that the first time grass appeared in New York?

Ginsberg: Well, for me anyway. Burroughs had had some in the heydays, gaydays of East St. Louis toodleloo.

Solomon: Ronnie Gold and I used to eat benny inhalers in about '49.

Ginsberg: That's what Kerouac used a lot for writing at first, too. And that's what Joan Burroughs took, but she was taking two or three inhalers a day, finally, when we were all living together a little later.

Int: In what other ways did Burroughs influence you?

Ginsberg: With books: Kafka, Korzybski's SCIENCE AND SANITY, Spengler's DECLINE OF THE WEST which he gave Kerouac, Blake, Rimbaud, Yeats's A VISION, Cocteau's OPIUM.

Solomon: Melville?

Ginsberg: No, that was Jack's interest. Especially, a little later, PIERRE, because of the euphuistic, packed poetical Shakespearean quality of the prose.

Int: And the Gothicism. Were there other books?

Ginsberg: Yes. Celine's JOURNEY TO THE END OF THE NIGHT, Auden, Hart Crane, and Eliot which I borrowed. It was my first introduction to modern literature really, and also to modern ideas.

Int: Would you say there were similarities between Eliot and Burroughs?

Ginsberg: St. Louis origins, yes. Going to England finally. They also had the same banker look

WSB under tree   photograph by Allen Ginsberg

which Bill always had but which he cultivated more later on. Bill actually applied to be in the O.S.S. because he knew Wild Bill Donovan from Harvard, and he was of that elite aristocracy that would have fitted into it, except that he had some early record of having cut off his little finger with a chicken shears to see what it was like.

Solomon: Wasn't that to get out of the service?

Ginsberg: And Bill's hatred of the American secret-police-bureaucracy grows from the fact that they wouldn't have him in it. I mean he knows them, that social type and mind.

Int: When were you introduced to gnostic ideas?

Ginsberg: The first time I heard the word gnostic mentioned was when Kerouac and I went to see Raymond Weaver, at Columbia, who had done the first biography of Melville, HERMAN MELVILLE: MARINER AND MYSTIC, and had discovered the text of BILLY BUDD. Weaver was this great scholar who shared an office with Mark Van Doren, adn Jack brought Weaver a novel called THE SEA IS MY BROTHER, his first poetical novel, and Weaver gave him a little list of books to read, like the EGYPTIAN GNOSTICS and either the TIBETAN BOOK OF THE DEAD or the EGYPTIAN BOOK OF THE DEAD, I can't remember.

Solomon: Burroughs's first contact with me was when he read my first article. He said the insights were psychological and not deep psychic.

Int: I felt Burroughs's influence in your last book, THE FALL OF AMERICA.

Ginsberg: Thematically, yes. But technically, Bunting, saying to condense more, that I had "too many words," getting rid of extra syntactical fat allows more perfume to verbs and nouns.

Taking Aim   photograph by Jon Blumb

Int: How come you chose as your Preface to FALL OF AMERICA that selection from Whitman's DEMOCRATIC VISTAS on adhesiveness? It seemed so ironic?

Ginsberg: Except that it does point to a goal and an ideal and a human potentiality that America was supposed to fulfill because that was the prophecy, the need, and the psychological condition of American democracy, and Whitman named it and particularized it very clearly in that passage. Also it gives credence, historical background, and traditional justification to my own adhesive poems.

Solomon: I was interested when I read FALL mainly in the sex, being a Bronx boy.

Int: In the tender obscenity of poems like "Please Master"?

Solomon: And "Graffiti."

Int: "Jessore Road" is especially Blakean, its metric, rhyme scheme, and the whole feeling of the poem like a long extended "London."

Ginsberg: The consequence of three years working on Blake songs. It was the first poem I wrote to music with chords, intended to be chanted and sung. I had finished two albums of Blake's INNOCENCE AND EXPERIENCE.

Int: I think I saw you singing the poem on television last year with a whole room of people?

Ginsberg: Yeah. With Dylan and Happy Traum. I wrote "Jessore Road" to have something really sublime to present to Dylan to record. So the performance that you saw on TV was a first performance without any rehearsal because I had finished typing the poem that afternoon, and I had written it the day before.

Int: You have written a number of poems in a very short period of time, haven't you? Didn't you write "Sunflower Sutra" while Kerouac was impatiently standing at your door waiting for you?

Ginsberg: Also poems like "A Strange New Cottage in Berkeley" and "Supermarket in California" which incidentally were part of one composition, and later cut apart.

Int: How were you affected by Kerouac's notion of no revision?

Ginsberg: "Sunflower Sutra" is almost completely untouched from the original. It took me a long time to get on to Kerouac's idea of writing without revision. I did it by going to his house where he sat me down with typewriter and said, "Just write a poem!" So I did about the Statue of Liberty, which I never published because it wasn't any good. But I did get the idea of how interesting it could be, the accidents that come up if you commit yourself irrevocably to accepting the traces of your mind during the composition.

Int: What led you to your concept of "undifferentiated consciousness"?

Ginsberg: Blake.

Int: The experience in 1948?

Ginsberg: Which convinced me that it was possible - just like the Cezanne thing, reproducing the petits sensations of experience. That's why I became interested in Cezanne after Blake, because when I looked at his painting I got a sudden shock of eternal thrill, that sensation of eternal space being reconstituted - but the experience of Blake was that through poetry you could catalyze in the reader the experience of Pater Omnipotens Eterna Deus, an experience of eternal consciousness; but then later on, reading Zen and other philosophy, I would find different nomenclature for it.

Int: In which of your own poems do you think you've come closest to achieving this quality?

Ginsberg: I don't know because it seems to happen accidentally, but apparently in HOWL where it is sufficient to alter people's minds.

Int: What about poems like "Journal Night Thoughts" or "Television Was A Baby Crawling Toward That Deathchamber"?

Ginsberg: No, that's like a full chaotic consciousness. There is too much excitement and activity in the consciousness, that's amphetamine partly. So it depends on what we mean by "undifferentiated consciousness".... but if we mean empty, Sunyata, in which everything comes in quietly, simultaneously, then I don't think I've written anything quiet enough for that...but to get enough excitement to break people's mind systems open, through rhythmic means partly, HOWL works.

Int: Burroughs was interested in conditioning, wasn't he?

Ginsberg: Yeah. Another book that he gave us at that early time was a book by someone named Jacobson called PROGRESSIVE RELAX-ATION which was a sort of Western homemade yoga - just lie down and begin untensing your whole body from the skull to the toes, muscle by muscle and portion by portion, which is similar to the Satipatthhana, or body-feeling-mind and mind-object meditation of Burmese Buddhists, which is primary Hinayana Buddhist Yoga.

Int: What about word conditioning?

Ginsberg: That was covered by Korzybski's SCIENCE AND SANITY immediately when he pointed out that words were not identical to the things that they represent. And the best example of that was when Lucien Carr and I had this big argument as to whether if you carved a walking stick on the moon, was it art or not? Burroughs said, "I never heard of such a stupid question!" In other words, art is whatever you want to define it as, it's only a three-letter word. Burroughs's attitude was that we were giving the word an essential identity outside of any use we might make of it, so if we wanted to use the word art to describe the walking stick on the moon, then it was art, and if we didn't want to use the word art, it wasn't. He just said: "It's too starved an argument for my sword," so he cut through arbitrary conceptions like a Zen master. It's like the goose in the bottle koan: if you put a full-grown goose inside a bottle with a narrow neck, how do you get the goose out without breaking the bottle, or damaging or bruising the goose? That's

That's one of the first koans that you meditate on if you're studying Zen. Another is the koan "Does the dog have a Buddha nature" the Zen master Jo-jo was once asked, and he answered, "Wu," which means no in Chinese. Why did Jo-jo say Wu?...Well how do you get the goose out?

Int: I don't know. How?

William's canes in a stand in his living room   photograph by Lee Ranaldo

Ginsberg: (claps hands loudly) It's out! Same way you put it in, with words. It's only a conceptual bottle. So Burroughs resolved the problem of whether a walking stick on the moon was art or not in exactly the same way.

Int: Did Pound reinforce this approach to language?

Ginsberg: I hadn't started reading Pound then.

Int: What about when you visited him in '67? Was he talking then?

Ginsberg: A little bit, in answer to very specific questions. I have a journal I kept on that which should appear in the next CITY LIGHTS JOURNAL. I wrote it a long time back, and gave it to Laughlin [James Laughlin, publisher of New Directions], and he sent it to Olga Rudge who got upset, and I couldn't at first figure out over what. Laughlin said it was because I had mentioned in the journal about how I had smoked a stick of grass at the table on Pound's eighty-first birthday. Then I saw Olga Rudge earlier this year in London, and apparently she objected to my quoting something Pound said to me. He said, "THE CANTOS are a mess, stupidity and ignorance all the way through, and the worst stupidity was stupid, suburban anti-Semitic prejudice."

Int: Why did she object to that? I mean, had Pound said it?

Ginsberg: Uh hum. But she maintained that Pound was not anti-Semitic, and it was a misunderstanding to think of him as anti-Semitic in the beginning.

Int: Was Pound's statement an apology?

Ginsberg: Well, she didn't want to see it as an apologia, and it wasn't precisely, I think, he was just being generous and extraordinarily sociable, and Prospero-like, taking some of the burden.

Int: I know how important Buddhism is in connection with your own work and Kerouac's, but is there any connection to Burroughs's?

Ginsberg: There is often an emphasis on open blue space like nirvana or transcendence, of conceptual mind prison...especially in his recent work, the idea of empty space in every direction which is very similar to the Buddhist view of Sunyata, oddly enough. "Out of the body experience," or "escape from the frightened, nagging, aging flesh" - that's Burroughs's phrase - is like the Buddhist view of release or moksha, liberation from impermanence, from metamorphosis into an unconditioned beginningless and endless suchness, nirvana - But Bill wouldn't go for nirvana, as it were, he would see that as a con. But nonetheless what he seems to be after recently, and I think it was implicit all along, is another modality or plane of consciousness where view is unconditioned. The images in all of the books following NAKED LUNCH, like "the blue tide" that comes in on yage, or the idea of "rub out the word," "all out of the body and into space," as at the end of the YAGE LETTERS, indicate a place that is very similar to the infinite spaciousness of Tibetan Buddhism.

Int: Still isn't this search, no matter what its end, conducted along a corridor of brutal self-immolation and explosions of pain?

Ginsberg: In one view that pain is part of the "apparent thought, feeling, and sensory phenomena," but Burroughs's late theory is that there's a squeeze on the body by a virus coming from Venus to make it as painful a place as possible, purposely contracting everybody into limited space, so Burroughs's remedy is unlimited space.

Solomon: Did Burroughs and Genet have conversations when they met in Chicago?

Ginsberg: Yes, a lot of conversation, I was with them. They loved each other and cared for each other, Bill talked a lot and Genet listened and laughed a lot, and told me Burroughs was very sweet and tender.

Solomon: We once characterized Burroughs as the American Genet.

Ginsberg: Genet told me he had read Burroughs in French, and that he liked his work and his person, and they went around in taxicabs together and marched together in tear-gas situations.

Solomon: What happened then, Genet escaped into the sewer or something?

Ginsberg: No, the guards said that we had to disperse: So David Dellinger, who was negotiating with the guards, called me up to chant mantras to keep everything quiet which I did for about twenty minutes in this tight situation. Then Dellinger announced that we had been ordered to disperse. We felt we had a legal right to stay, all those who wanted to leave could and the rest would invoke passive resistance, sit on the ground and offer themselves for arrest. Genet, being in the country illegally, having come in through the Canadian border, had to cut. So I think Richard Seaver took Genet away, and Burroughs and I stayed....And Genet gave a speech to the Yippies saying that he hoped that some day the skyline of Chicago would be covered with vines, that he felt it was necessary for writers to be with the younger people in body as well as sympathy.

Solomon: I remember reading that Genet said at that time that he had had much experience eluding the police so it was nothing for him.

Jewel-encrusted knives, skulls and other objects   photograph by Lee Ranaldo

Int: I'd like to return to Burroughs's theory of evil. What would you say is its source?

Ginsberg: Well, originally it was analyzed by William Lee, the factualist (perhaps representative of a trust of giant insects from another galaxy) in

NAKED LUNCH. But since then, in NOVA EXPRESS and TICKET THAT EXPLODED, and more recently in EXTERMINATOR! and THE JOB and WILD BOYS, the agency of the hallucinating Word is a virus from Venus so it's not other galaxies anymore - it's an external, extraterrestrial threat from within our own solar system.

Int: Would you go along with the notion that madness is the norm in Burroughs's fiction?

Ginsberg: I would say the norm is metamorphosis. In Burroughs's fiction, madness is the normal behavior of the political world, but it's also a medium that A.J. Benway and the factualists are able to handle and deal with and use as the material for their examination...and sometimes get caught in as is possible for an explorer to get caught in a sticky wicket, or as Burroughs himself feels that he has been caught in certain areas that he could not handle with drugs like psylocybin and LSD, or yage originally. But madness is not his ultimate goal, just the obstacle. This is why Burroughs's geography is so similar to gnostic and Tibetan procedural maps. The wrathful deities are the guardians of the gate to Sunyata, blue space...except Burroughs is ascribing all these wrathful deities to a plot by the Control Forces. So his books really are investigations of his consciousness to "trace along the word lines" to the source of the control.

Int: So he has a greater conspiratorial sense of history than even you do, I guess?

Ginsberg: Mine is a little more mundane like investigations of CIA involvement with dope trafficking in Indochina (which was I think a successful investigation).

Int: What about applying Longfellow's remark on the transcendentalist utopians, that they expressed the "divine insanity of noble minds"?

Ginsberg: I think Burroughs would reject that as sentimental rhetoric because he feels that he is more of a precise scientist investigating

60

regions of consciousness forbidden to common understanding by the Control agencies, and the danger of such investigation is physical pain, madness, "the Ovens," but the factualist investigator armed with various antivirus exercises such as rubbing out the word can ultimately resist, though there may be certain aspects which you can't resist...and what you can't resist that most dismays him at present comes in the phrase "At Hiroshima all was lost"...or so he said this year when I went to see him to find out what he was thinking lately. He said that the project was to get out of the body - as the soul or spirit gets out of the body - but that the problem with the atom bomb is that its temperature is so high that it's a killer of souls." So human beings have arrived at a situation where they can be the Killer of Souls. So I said, traditionally, with the gnostics or Buddhists, there is no soul to kill, the void is impervious to the meta-physical heat of the bomb. He answered that all that Buddhist and Hindu mythology was very amateur, compared with the kind of precise investigations that might be conducted now in a highly chemical and technological age. For Burroughs, yoga and Buddhism are primitive methods of achieving detachment; it can now be done more immediately through electronic means.

Int: But less intuitional.

Ginsberg: Well, just as he uses the physical table as a place to put his mind to cut up, putting the words on the table rather than inner meditation only - so he sees mechanical aids, like a Yankee inventor, as being a possibility; and also he says we can't turn back, we've already advanced into a highly mechanized, electronic dimension, and that may be the Path. So he puts down the rural commune back-to-nature aspect of what Gary Snyder and myself are doing, saying that it's retrogressive, that we're too deeply plunged into the science fiction reality situation now. For Burroughs the problem is not so much the fact of science or experiment, as it is that it's being controlled, that secrets are being kept - like the Army is the only one that has real license to experiment with acid anymore and maybe scientology is another extension of the CIA network. So his idea is "All secrets out" now.

Int: So resistance becomes openness?

Ginsberg: Right, by making use of secret material and turning it against Control Agencies, and by realizing that there are a few simple principles of technology that everyone can understand and master which have been obscured by the authoritarian Controllers. That's why he's been experimenting with the cutting up of sounds and playing them back, in other words feeding back the control images to the Control Central in the hope of setting up anti-image consciousness feedback that will explode their Control machine.

WSB in backyard   photograph by Allen Ginsberg

Int: That's in THE TICKET THAT EXPLODED.

Ginsberg: And which he practiced at Chicago when he came into the Convention Hall with his tape recorder with all sorts of riot sounds from Tangiers like shutters slamming and started spraying all these sounds out on the balcony of the convention, and within an hour the place was in an uproar.

Int: Is the terrifying chaos in Burroughs's fiction purposeful?

Ginsberg: I think so. He would maintain that he is making propositions and hypotheses which he examines by means of language and imagination. So chaos - transfiguration is a better word, really - is only the preliminary guardian of the sacred extraterrestrial area of consciousness. The end is not dereglement de tous les sens but clear vision, not chaos but total silence and calm like a great blue tide flooding the body. And dereglement de tous les sens is not even so much a means as it is a by-product of the pursuit through to the other side of phenomena, the disruption of the apparently normal order determined by the CIA and the Control Forces. In fact he feels that they are responsible for the chaotic apparitions, the fear, the Ovens, the images of death. What he is saying over and over, also, is that death is the greatest con, that it has been created by the Controllers to scare everybody, and there's really nothing to fear.

Int: Is he still involved with the scientologists?

Ginsberg: Only in denouncing them, he wrote a long attack on them as a fascist organization in ROLLING STONE. I went to supper with him and Girodias and heard another terror story about the scientologists - which is that Girodias published a book attacking scientology, and they sued him to try and stop the book and they lost the suit, so they organized a letter-writing campaign to the British Home Office complaining that Girodias was a pornographer, and so the Police raided Girodias and seized 125,000 volumes and drove him out of business in England. So he couldn't defend himself because his assets had been seized. And many things like that have happened, so Burroughs has attacked the scientologists as an extension of the control apparatus that offers people hints of exercises that are useful, but which hangs them up in the middle of the exercise.

Int: How does Burroughs see his own function as a writer relating to this control system?

Ginsberg: The virus from venus (as before a trust of giant insects from another galaxy) or as in other times the CIA, or the economic control monopolists, or the antisex forces, are all resumed in terms of Power Addiction. So Burroughs wants to discover the source where the original imposition of brainwash comes from. He sees his job also as an explorer and inventor of how-to books, how to combat brainwash, how to liberate consciousness from the conditions imposed on it by the Control Forces.

Int: So if the reader can read his books, he is along the way to violating that conditioning by virtue of experiencing Burroughs's own techniques, just as the readers who read THE WASTE LAND learned a new kind of perception?

Spray Can Man   photograph by Jon Blumb

Ginsberg: Yes. Throughout his books there are all these suggestions on how to observe your own speech and behavior to see who were the people who influenced you and to trace your attitudes, gestures, styles, words, and tones of voice to the original people you were imitating, your father, teachers, lovers, or whoever was leaving an impression on you. Last time I saw him he told me that "whoever leaves an impression on you is a vampire." His statement was so impressive...striking I mean...curious...that I went home that night and had a dream of William Blake as a vampire because Blake had in a sense invaded my consciousness, left an impression which struck me and stuck me there revolving around the corpse of that impression for decades...which was a violation of the Tantric injunction not to cling to any impression. So Burroughs is saying that for his own role he wants to make "himself" obsolete.

William S. Burroughs and silhouette   photograph by Allen Ginsberg

THE TICKET IS EXPLODING

by Ron Whitehead

with suffering comes humility
and with it
in the end
wisdom
— *J. Swift*

RW: Why did you decide to settle in Algiers which at that time was home to various military bases rather than one of the traditional bohemian neighborhoods?

WSB: Yes because it was a hell of a lot cheaper. Real estate there was cheapest. I got that house for $7,000 something.

RW: Any memories of different New Orleans neighborhoods you visited, music, riding the ferry?

WSB: The Quarter, strange plays, didn't get around too much.

RW: The New Orleans Police have come under attack recently, imagine that, for corruption. A cop hired executioners to kill a woman who signed a brutality complaint against him. Louisiana police cars have So

67

No One Will Have To Fear inscribed on sides. Do you have any observations about The New Orleans Police, about the illegal search of your home there, firearms they confiscated?

WSB: No. They never laid a finger on me as far as any brutality goes. They did lead me to believe that one of them was a Federal agent when he wasn't. He was a City cop. So there was an illegal search. But I didn't know it at the time. The next day I was arrested. There was someone with me I hardly knew. He was just introduced to me. He had one joint on him. He'd thrown out larger amounts but had one and they found it right away. Then the next day they went in and took my car and I never got it back, though I wasn't convicted of anything. See they can confiscate your property even though you're not convicted of anything. And that's really scary sinister.

RW: Both our political parties are looking like a bird with two right wings....

WSB: Exactly.

RW: The Police are gaining more powers daily as our personal freedoms are disappearing

WSB: See that's what I say. The whole drug war is nothing but a pretext to increase Police power and personnel and that of course is dead wrong. So many created imag-

WSB in Gun Shop   photograph by Allen Ginsberg

ined drug offenses.

RW: New Orleans has North America's largest magical community. In recent years you've spoken bluntly about your interest in magic. In New Orleans did you encounter magic in any form?

WSB: No I didn't.

RW: Do you see any irony in having a literary marker commemorate your 509 Wagner Street, Algiers home, a place where you lived briefly, perhaps unhappily. Did you produce any writing there?

WSB: Oh yes, quite a bit. And I wouldn't say I was particularly unhappy there.

RW: So it wasn't that bad?

WSB: No it wasn't. Not at all.

RW: Jack Kerouac spent a large section of ON THE ROAD, pages 141-156 Viking, on the New Orleans visit.

WSB: Oh well Kerouac was writing fiction. What he did when he wrote about me...he made me out with Russian Countesses and Swiss accounts and other things I didn't have or didn't happen and so on. Yet... some truth, some fiction.

RW: You have dramatically influenced Music, Literature, Film, Art, Advertising, Culture in General. Are you intrigued by that influence? How did you first become conscious of other people's perception of you as an icon?

WSB: Well, slowly of course. Over time. Reading the paper, magazines, journals, that sort of thing.

RW: The request for interviews becomes absurd after a while. This is first and last one I intend to do. I feel uncomfortable in position of interviewer.

WSB: Yes, it becomes absurd because interviewers generally ask the same questions say the same things.

RW: Recently you've been barraged with interview requests especially in relation to the deaths of Timothy Leary and Jan Kerouac.

WSB: Yes, of course, I knew Leary, but barely knew didn't really know Jan. James knew her, was friends with her, but I didn't.

RW: Hunter S. Thompson, who I like so much, is, like me, from Louisville, Kentucky, and you're from just up the road in St.Louis. I recently visited Hunter at his home in Colorado. Hunter said he thought he was a pretty good shot until he went shooting with you.

WSB: I'll put it like this: some days you're good and some you aren't.

W.S.B. w/.44 Special S&W   photograph by Jon Blumb

RW: You must have been good that day. Hunter was real impressed.

WSB: Well, he gave me a great pistol.

RW: Like Hunter, some people would say that you're a Southern Gentleman with a world literary reputation but both you and Hunter have escaped the Southern Writer label. Any comments?

WSB: I escaped the label because I didn't and don't write about the South.

RW: Do you have a personal favorite of your own readings? I know you've been in the studio recording JUNKY.

Recording   photograph by Jon Blumb

WSB: No, I don't have any special favorite.

RW: Other than Brion Gysin is there anyone you miss the most?

WSB: When you get my age there are more and more people you know, have known, that you miss. Brion, Antony Balch, Ian Summerville are ones I think of right away, I was quite close to.

RW: Diane di Prima is underrated underappreciated in world today. Her autobiography will be released by Viking Penguin. I hope she'll finally receive credit that's long overdue.

Reading in Lawrence, Kansas   photograph by Jon Blumb

WSB: Yes, I hope so too.

RW: You've had much to say about Samuel Beckett. Beckett's mentor, James Joyce, was an anarchist who devoted his life work to undermining deconstructing the dominant paradigm of patriarchy in government, religion, family, literature. I'm doing research asking The Beats what influence James Joyce had, if any, on their writing. How do you feel about Joyce?

WSB: Well he's great, a very great writer. Any modern writer is bound to be influenced by Joyce. Of course, by Beckett as well.

RW: I had a long conversation with Allen Ginsberg about Bob Dylan. Allen talked about his personal feelings towards Dylan and also about Dylan's work. Allen said he felt like Dylan would be remembered long after The Beats and he added reasons why. This is a strong statement especially coming from Allen Ginsberg. Do you have any comments on this?

WSB: No, no I don't. Not in any cursory way. Of course, I've listened to and know his music and met him a couple of times but I don't have any strong statements to make.

RW: How much are you able to keep up with music today?

WSB: Some much more than others. I've worked with and am very good friends with Patti Smith and Jim Carroll.

RW: How do you feel about this historic marker?

WSB: Fine. Fine. It's an honor like the French Commandeur de l'Ordre des Arts et des Lettres. Commander of Arts and Letters. Commander of Arts and Letters.

Calling The Toads

Hummmm Hummmm

Hummmm

Hummmm

Hummmm

Hummmm

Hummmm
Hummmm

Calling the toads
Calling the toads
We shall come rejoicing
Calling the toads

one step out the door off the step
goin down swingin
in a peyote amphetamine benzedrine
dream
I'm five years old I am the messenger holdin
William Burroughs Bill Burroughs
Old Bull Lee's hand
holdin Bill's hand on some lonely
godforsakinuppermiddleclassSt.Louisstreet
and we're hummin' we're hummin'
we're hummin' in tones
we're hummin' in tones
callin' the toads
oh yeah were callin' the toads
Bill's eyes twinklin glitterin'
a devilish grin crackin' the corners
of his mouth and I'm lookin' him
right smack in the eyes
deep in the eyes I'm readin'
his heroined heart yes I'm readin' his old heart
but it ain't the story I expected
as we move this way and that
raisin' and lowerin' our heads our voices
callin' the toads
and here they come
marchin' high and low from
under the steps from under
the shrooms from the front yard
from round the corner of the house
fallin' from the trees
rainin' down here come the toads
all sizes and shapes all swingin'
and swayin' and dancin' that
magic Burroughs Beat
yes here come the toads singin'

and swayin' and swingin' their hips
now standin' all round us hundreds thousands of toads
eyes bulgin' tongues stickin' out hard
dancin' a strange happy vulgar rhythmed
dance for Burroughs and me
yes Burroughs yes Burroughs
yes Burroughs I see his heart
and I know his secret
a secret noone has discovered
til now but I'll never tell
never reveal as I witness
this sacred scene this holy ceremony
this gathering
this universal song and dance
I witness through the eyes the heart
of William S. Burroughs
King of the Toads

Calling the toads
Calling the toads
We shall come rejoicing
Calling the toads
hummmm

William on his front porch   photograph by Lee Ranaldo

WILLIAM S. BURROUGHS I-View

by Lee Ranaldo

In April 1997 I had the chance to connect via telephone with William Burroughs to ask him some questions about Morocco and the years he spent in Tanger. Having traveled there a few times myself recently, I was curious about the Maroc of the forties and fifties, when Tanger was classified an "International Zone" and the laws were famously lax. We spoke for about half an hour that afternoon—I got the impression William wasn't really up for much more than that; he was alert but sounding a bit weary.

It wasn't until some months later in a Kaatskill Mountain cabin that I dug out the cassette tape to transcribe. I spent the better part of that afternoon trying to decipher his gravelly drawl, and pondering his life's journey. On two occasions Sonic Youth had the opportunity to visit him at his home in Lawrence, Kansas, where he took great pleasure in showing us jewel-encrusted knives, gun catalogues, his beloved cats, and the Orgone box out back which he'd built himself, between the pond and garden. Two days later on August 2 I heard of his death. I felt I had just been conversing with him. Barely three months separated his death from that of his lifelong friend Allen Ginsberg.

Allen Ginsberg photographing Lee Ranaldo   photograph by Gordon Ball

This man, who spoke of *language as a virus*, had become sublim-
inal, a skewed organism, rooting under the cultural skin of our time.
Imagine a world un-cut-up, without his bone-dry timing, without The
Soft Machine or Dr. Benway. Imagine how much vital, challenging work
from the last few decades, in so many fields, might not exist without him.

Later in the month, when *The New Yorker* published his final
journal entries, it was clear that he could see the end coming. And what
was he left with? Here is his final entry, day before he died: *"Love? What
is it? Most natural painkiller. What there is. LOVE."* Those are the
thoughts he leapt off with. Even before the words make sense, that voice
is digging in. Listen to him speak yr mind, find rock power writ in his
pages, let yr fingernails be left uncleaned.

—LR 10/97

loud dial tone and faint "hello, hello?"
silence
touch tone phone tones
ringing 5 or 6 times

WSB: eh, Hello?

LR: Is this William?

WSB: Yeah.

LR: Hi William, this is Lee Ranaldo in New York City.

WSB: Yeah.

LR: How are ya?

WSB: Oh… okay.

LR: Well you sound pretty good.

(static)

LR: Okay, I wanted to talk to you, for just a few minutes this after-noon, about Morocco, if you would…

WSB: Just a moment, I gotta get my drink…

LR: Okay.

(25 sec silence)

WSB: OK.

LR: Okay, first off, William, I'd like to say that I was very sad to hear about Allen—I know you guys have been friends for the longest time…

WSB: Yes. Yes, well he knew, he knew it. He faced it.

LR: It seems like he faced it in a very dignified way, actually.

WSB: Yep, he told me — "I thought I'd be terrified but I'm not at all . . ."

LR: He did?

WSB: Yes—"I'm exhilarated!" he said.

LR: Well, I suppose if anyone had the right, uh, frame about them to go out that way, it was probably him. I was hoping to get one more visit in with him before he passed on, but that was not meant to be. I'm sure a lot of people felt the same. When was the last time you saw him?

WSB: Los Angeles. At my show there.

LR: I wanted to talk to you about Morocco a little bit. I've recently been to the country, a few times, and done some exploring, and I know you spent quite a bit of time in Tanger. I just wanted to pick yr brain about that a little bit. You went to Tanger for the first time in 1953, 1954?

WSB: Nineteen… fifty–four, I believe.

LR: How did you end up in Morocco? What was it about the place that drew you there? I mean, today there are a lot of different romantic associations with the coast of North Africa…

WSB: There were a lot more then than there are now, I can tell you that. You'll notice more subdivisions now, as it's modernized and is no longer cheap. For one thing, it was *very* cheap then. Yeah, man, I lived like a king for $200 a month.

LR: Did it have the same sort of appeal, then, that Berlin had in the sixties and seventies—an international zone of sorts?

WSB: Pretty much so. It was an anything goes place, and that's anoth-

By William's Fish Pool   photograph by Lee Ranaldo

er plus.

LR: And that was pretty available knowledge, when you went there?

WSB: Oh sure.

LR: Had you known Paul Bowles, or known about him, before you went there?

WSB: I'd read his books. I didn't know him.

LR: Did you meet him fairly quickly after you were there?

WSB: Mmm, I'd been there for some time, I'd met him very slightly. Later we became quite good friends—but that was some years afterwards.

LR: Do you enjoy his writing?

WSB: Very much, very much. Very particular style—particularly in the *end* of *Let It Come Down*, that's terrific—terrific; and *The Sheltering Sky* is almost a perfect novel. The end of that, oh man, that quote: *"At the end of the Arab quarter the car stopped; it was the end of the line."*—great!

LR: Did you know Jane (Bowles)?

WSB: Oh yes, quite well.

LR: What'd you think of her?

WSB: Oh she was incredible…

LR: I've heard incredible things about her—she lived quite an interesting life herself, although I guess in general women in Morocco were very much invisible, in a certain way. Native women, at least…

Soft Boy   photograph by Felver

WSB: It's a very complicated situation, very complex, and I don't pretend to know much about it. Jane Bowles was sort of known for her strange behavior. In New York they invited her to some party where all these powerful ladies were, and they asked her, "Mrs. Bowles, what do you think of all this?", and she said "Oh" and fell to the floor in quite a genuine faint. That was her answer!

LR: Did you pretty much exist within an expatriate community there, or did you have a lot of contact with the local people? Was is easy to have contact?

WSB: The local people—umm, I don't speak a fuckin' word of Arabic, but I speak a little Spanish—y'know, they all spoke Spanish in the Northern Zone. My relations were mostly with the Spanish. Spanish boys. And, of course, otherwise in the expatriate side.

LR: Right, but you didn't frequent the Barbara Hutton crowd?

WSB: Nooo.

LR: There was a description, in Barry Miles book *(El Hombre Invisible)*, where he said that you felt very lonely and cut off, being isolated in this corner of North Africa—

WSB: It wasn't being in a corner of North Africa that made it so, it was the fact that I hadn't made many friends there.

LR: Was that a strange time for you? Living there without really knowing anyone?

WSB: Not particularly, I've visited many places alone, many times...

LR: Do you think that the general tenor of life in Morocco influenced the way you were writing at that point? The daily life coming out in some of the routines?

WSB: Probably. The more I was in that surrounding the more I liked it. More and more. Yeah—it was cheap—and then, I met this guy Dave Ulmer *(?)*, who was Barnaby Bliss *(his nom de plume)*. He was at work writing society columns for the Tanger paper—an English (language) paper, the *Morocco Courier*—run by an old expatriate named

Byrd, William Byrd, an old Paris expat. [Ulmer/Bliss, a character of some unsavory repute, supposedly introduced WSB to Tanger's young boy homo–sex scene, and also, more importantly, to Paul Bowles—LR]

LR: Did you do much traveling around Morocco while you were there, or did you pretty much just stick in Tanger?

WSB: I'm ashamed to say, not much. I went to Fes, I went to Marrakech, and passed through Casablanca, some other places there—I forget the names of the coastal towns... and I've been to Jajouka!

LR: Yeah, I wanted to talk to you about that—I'm friendly with Bachir Attar, and the last time we were there I went to Jajouka as well... I saw your inscriptions in his big scrapbook, and heard some stories—

WSB: Yeah.

LR: How did you end up there?

WSB: Through Brion Gysin, more or less.

LR: What did you make of the music?

WSB: Great, great. I loved it. Magic—it really has a magical quality that you can't find anymore, anywhere. It's dying out everywhere, that quality...

LR: It still seems to be in evidence when they play today— I don't know if you've heard them recently...

WSB: Not recently, but I've heard the recordings, some of the recordings. Ornette Coleman made some, you know. I was there when he made those.

LR: Excuse me?

WSB: I was there.

LR: You were there when he made those *(Dancing in Your Head)* recordings?

WSB: That's right.

Kim Gordon, Michael Stipe and William   photograph by Lee Ranaldo

LR:

Oh, gee, wasn't that in the 70's? I didn't know you were there when those recordings were happening…

WSB: Yeah, it was, '72, I think.

LR: Are you still in touch with Bachir?

WSB: No, not really.

LR: You were in touch with his father, I suppose…

WSB: Yes, I knew the old man, sure, I remember him. He was the leader of the group back then.

LR: How many musicians would you say were in the group back then?
WSB: Oh, I don't know, it would vary, I'd say about 12, 15.

William with Thurston and Coco Moore   photograph by Lee Ranaldo

LR: That's about how many there are today as well. What about at the 1001 Nights *(Gysin's restaurant in Tanger)*—were the Jajouka musicians playing in there?

WSB: Well, various musicians. They had dancing boys in there, too. But I didn't know Brion too well—I was only there a couple of times. I didn't know him then. I became friendly with him in Paris, later.

LR: Were you involved much with the music there, in Morocco—in Tanger? Did it make any strong impression on you?

WSB: Well, I like the Moroccan music very much—the music is omnipresent. I'd be sitting at my desk and hear it outside. It was all around you.

LR: I'd like to hear your impressions of the *kif* smoking there, and the *majoun*—

WSB: Sure. Well, the *kif* smoking was, y'know, anywhere and every-where. There were no laws...

LR: They sort of smoke it the way people have a drink here, as a social relaxant?

WSB: Well, not exactly the same way. In the first place—it's pretty much confined to men, though I suppose the women get to smoke on their own. But anyway, of course *majoun* is just a candy made from *kif*—the *kif*, you see, is mixed with tobacco—

LR: Right.

WSB: I can't smoke it.

LR: Nope.

WSB: So I'd always get those boys with the tobacco, I'd tell 'em: 'I don't want the tobacco in it.' So I rolled my own, and made my own *majoun*. It's just a candy, it's pretty much like a Christmas pudding—any sort of candy works good, fudge or whatever.

LR: And how did you find it? Was the high pretty pleasing?

WSB: Very very very much. It was stronger than pot.

LR: Were you smoking a lot of that, or taking a lot of that, when you were writing some of the routines?

87

WSB: Yeah, sure. It helped me alot.

LR: The place where you spent a lot of your time there (in Tanger)—the Muniria *(the famed "Villa Delirium")*?

WSB: The Hotel Muniria, yes.

LR: Was it a hotel or a boarding house?

WSB: It was a hotel.

LR: That's where you wrote a lot of the routines that became Naked Lunch?

WSB: Quite a few of them, yes.

LR: And is that where Kerouac, Ginsberg and Orlovsky, those guys, came to visit you?

WSB: I was living there at that time, yes. They didn't—there wasn't a place in the Muniria, but they found various cheap places around very near there.

LR: I heard Kerouac had nightmares from typing up your stuff at that time…

WSB: *(pauses)* Well, *he* said…

LR: Was he the first one to actually sit down and type a bunch of that stuff up?

WSB: No, he was by no means the first. Alan Ansen did a lot of typing, and of course Allen Ginsberg. I don't know who was first but it wasn't Jack.

LR: Those guys came and went pretty quickly, compared with the amount of time you spent in Morocco—I guess they weren't as enamored of the place...

WSB: Well they were settled somewhere else. Now for example, Jack didn't like any place outside of America—he hated Tanger.

LR: I wonder why?

WSB: He hated Paris because they couldn't understand his French.

LR: His French was a Canadian dialect...

WSB: Those French Canadians got themselves into a *language ghetto*. Even the French people don't speak their language! Anyway, he'd been to Mexico quite a lot, more than many other places. He liked it there fairly well.

LR: But he didn't like it very much in Tanger?

WSB: No no, not at all.

LR: Was Tanger a violent place then?

WSB: It was never a violent place that I know of—never! Good God—I walked around in Tanger at all hours of the day and night, never any trouble. There's this idea that you go into the native quarter you immediately get stabbed—*(laughs)*—it's nonsense!

LR: Well, people do bring back those stories now and again...

WSB: Well, occasionally it happens, but it is much less dangerous that certain areas of New York—my God!

LR: If you can navigate the streets of New York you're in pretty good stead just about anywhere, I guess.

WSB: Yeah, that's right, you're much safer in Tanger than in New York.

LR: Were there many travelers or tourists in Morocco at that time?

photograph by Jon Blumb

WSB: Not many at all. It was nice. In the summer of course you had sometimes quite a few Scandinavians, Germans... *(laughs)* Brian Howard said about the Swedes, I think it was: 'You're all ugly, you're all queer, and none of you have any money!'

LR: There was another quote in Miles' book, you saying that you'd "…never seen so many people in one place without any money or the prospect of any money…"

WSB: You certainly could live cheaply there, yes.

LR: Did Americans have to register with the police to live there?

WSB: Of course not, nothing, they had to do nothing. Well, they put in various regulations in town—you had to get a card. By the time we got our goddamn cards and stood in line and had to take all that crap— I had to get one of those in France, too—well, anyway, by that time they had another idea *(laughs)*, so your card that you had acquired was worthless…

LR: When was the last time you were back in Morocco?

WSB: When in the hell was it? I went there with—the last time I went with Jeremy Thomas and David Cronenberg, apropos of possibly getting some shots, y'know…

LR: Oh, for the movie *(Naked Lunch)*?

WSB: Yeah, for the sets. Well, we just were there a couple of days. It had changed, not incredibly but considerably. There's been a lot of building up, a lot of sort of sub-divisions—it's gotten more westernized. There used to be a lot of good restaurants there, now there's only one, and that's in the Hotel Minza. These people I was with were saying 'Oh show me to a little place in the native quarter where the food is good…' and I said: 'There aren't no such places! Right here in your best food in Morocco, or in Tanger anyway, right in the Hotel Minza!' Well, they went out and they ate in an awful, greasy Spanish restaurant. After that they believed me!

LR: *(laughs) They* had to find out the hard way…

LR: Okay William, I think that that's gonna be good, that about covers the subjects I'd wanted to get at you with, on there…

WSB: Well fine.

Typewriter in Bill's Garden   photograph by Lee Ranaldo

LR: I appreciate your talking to me, it's a great pleasure to talk to you.

WSB: Well, it's my pleasure too.

LR: Okay, I hope to get another chance to come out and say hello to you out there in Lawrence—

WSB: That'd be fine.

LR: Y'know, I have one last question for you—is that, uh, typewriter still growing out in your garden?

WSB: *(puzzled)* What typewriter?

LR: Last time we were out there to visit, you had a typewriter growing in your garden amongst all the plants and things…

WSB: Oh, just one I threw away I guess…

LR: Yeah, it was a very beautiful image there, with the weeds coming up through the keys…

WSB: *(laughs)* I guess so—I don't remember the typewriter—I've gone through so many typewriters—wear 'em out and throw 'em away.

LR: Do you generally write with a computer these days?

WSB: I have no idea how to do it. No, I don't.

LR: Typewriter or longhand?

WSB: Typewriter or longhand, yes. These modern inventions! James *(Grauerholz)* has one, but I just don't.

LR: Okay, well listen William, I thank you very much. Please tell both Jim and James thanks for their help as well.

WSB: I certainly will.

LR: Okay, you take care.

WSB: You too.

LR: Bye bye.

WSB: Bye bye.

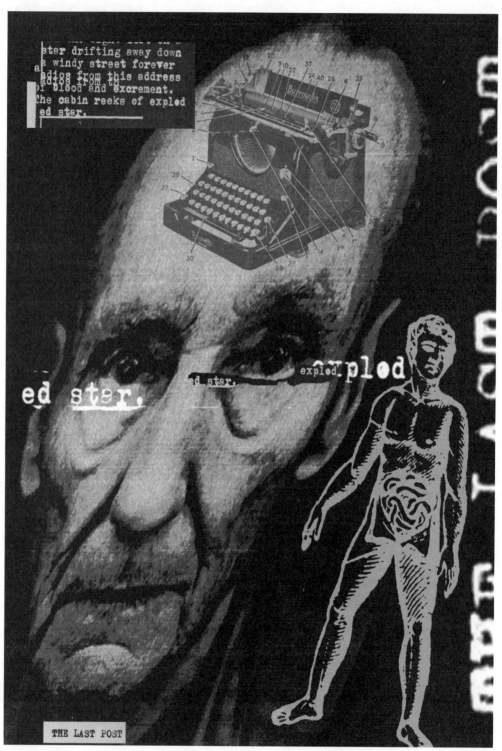

ster drifting away down
a windy street forever
ading from this address
f blood and excrement.
he cabin reeks of explod
ed star.

ed star.   ed star.   explod explod

THE LAST POST

the cabin reeks of exploded star   digital montage by rlmar

Autopsy

by Dee, MD, Fringecore Labs
& Tariq Zayid, Field Agent, Ring Tarigh

The body of the deceased William (Bill) Seward Burroughs (alias Lee, Old Bull, Claude etc.), born St Louis, 1914, was received today for examination at the Interzone mortuary. This is a summary of the autopsy findings.

Case History

Mr. B, 83 years old at time of death, renowned writer, performer, killer, visionary experimentalist, media manipulator, exploited genius, cantankerous, misogynous, homoerotic drug addict, was found de-energised and no longer contagious.

Death resulted from POT (post orgasmic tranquillity) overload, probably following long-term consummate bouts of The Sickness The Cold Burn, The Cold, Boredom, Body Load, Darting, agoraphilia, anisonogamy, intermittent commasculation, homilophilia, pecattiphilia and lascivious, obscene delirium.

Deceased was found in a Fugue state with total disorientation separating the cognitive part of his being

95

from the sensory part, which had long been desta-
bilised in a cocktail of highly concentrated acidic
bitterness and inflationary flashbacks, causing a
chronic dis-function to the sensory system, leading to
an exhilarating mis-belief in his own self-importance,
self-validation, noise overload and overexposure.

Baseline infinite. Wiring negative. Metabolism zero.
Immediately prior to death, deceased seemingly reached
Plus Four state of divine transformation, causing a
participation mystique and total connectedness with
both the interior and exterior universes. However,
subsequent analyses refute this.

External Examination

The body was found to be of a remarkably emaciated
adult male with a look of borrowed flesh resembling a
deconstructed sculpture of junkydom. The whole body
smelled of dry lust and displayed permanent cellular
alteration. Skin: dry, infested with blow flies -
feeding and laying eggs and hatching maggots, lustre-
less, eaten away in parts by acidic sweat rashes, virtually translucent, chronically pulpated, brownish
yellow, repeatedly consumed with needle marks, safety
pin marks, shot line marks, syrette marks, through
which the deceaseds soul has long since escaped; muscles slackened away from the bones, (as though the body
had been lying in salt water); what apparently had
been previously highly charged flesh, now appears more
as post-electrocution burn out. Fingers, like spongy
worms appropriate to searching out any orifice available. The face resembling that of a withered adoles-
cent, swollen under the eyes, which show acute mydri-
asis and although look like lifeless capsules of drea-
ry bitterness, still reflect the shining pearls of
lust inside. The lips thickened from the glandular
action of drugs. Pathological change to the backs of
the legs, neck and anal regions. The latter showing
signs of heavy abrasion, bruising, oedema and mucous
discharge and traces/smears of bloody faeces and spit-
tle. The anal muscles themselves were rather lax and
the orifice was also dilated and funnelled. Skull

unfiltered, likely 'Hardhead'. Genitals, gently crushed.

Internal examination and Histology

Upon opening, the body gives off a heavy metallic stench of brown blood, which resembles syrup. The body infested with piggybacked toxins : traces of morphine, heroine, dilaudid, eukodal, pantopon, diocodid, diosane, opium, demerol, dolophine, palfium, keif, marijuana/hashish, mescaline, bannisteria caapi, LSD6, Sacred mushrooms, MDMA, yage, ketamine, chlorophyll, apomorphine, cortizone, antihistamines, tranquillisers, tolsenol, reserpine, lubricants, and vegetable shortening. The spine rigid and stiff. The stomach showing signs of hunger : the sweet smell of gut decay, innards glistening. The reek of the emptied bowel is heightened by the overspill of urine. Liver weak. The brain chronically overheated, opened up, telepathic, infested with remorse intelligence, showing heavy traces of genius. The prostrate seemingly punched and enlarged, the sphincters and valves in the rectum scratched and stretched, colon and transverse colon showing signs of manipulation, anal muscles over-stretched. Rectal epithelium/cell wall generally damaged and infected with bacteria. Veins clearly mainlined. The presence of sub-endocardial haemorrhage in the heart confirmed. Possibly, brought about by the recent death of loved ones.

Discussion

It is clear from the external and internal examinations that the deceased was a spiritually overloaded, experimental genius, with traces of telepathic skill and at an earlier stage had been highly contagious and a major influence on cultural evolution. Due to the fact that the deceased became overcome by the Fugue state in recent times, he had taken to involving himself in harmful media activities, which impeded his useful functioning and led to serious character and

physical pathological states, causing unwarranted bitterness towards his fellow humans. However, when these
manifestations came into contact and disharmony with
lustful excesses and repetitive use of narcotics, hal-
lucinogens (which had been highly stimulative in early
life) and other substances, the psyche and the body
began to disintegrate. Hopefully prior to total
destruction, Mr. B. managed to reach Plus Four (++++)
state.

Dee, MD, Fringecore Labs.

0100101110100110100100101110100110100

Orgone Desiring Machine.

Field Notes, Assemblage Systemics, and Syntactic Evo-
lutionary Analysis of the Crime Scene ++ slg.b:
Subject: Mr. B. (E.H.I.)
Field Agent: Tariq Zayid

Ground Zero.

'All true freedom is dark and is infallibly identified with
sexual freedom, which is also dark, although we do not know
precisely why.'

Antonin Artaud

Same stimulus/same response. A humanity as a plane is
to fractal: objective illusion. To measure is to dis-
turb. We used to imagine that there was a real universe, outside of us, which could persist even when we
stopped observing it. The negation of the empirical
notion of antecedent observation: we can never catch
the world taking a holiday. Despite this realization
(subject) continued to construct and live out (subject's) world views, theologies, cosmologies in the
hope that we will see the truth of the matter.

Interrogation Documents: Love and Lust.

Int. File: 73-38.
"His particular sexual thing is being screwed, because
(subject) can come when he is screwed; he's one of the
few men that can"
"You mean without manipulating himself?"
"Yeah...look, no hands!"

Int. File: 85-165.
"That used to be one of Cocteau's party tricks — take
off all his clothes, lie down, and come off, no hands."

Every Opening is an Eye:
terminal portion and opening of the alimentary canal
of vertabrates and many invertebrates - in humans com-
prises the anal canal and opening, the end of the large
intestine - ·its function is to excrete fecal material
from the body - numerous blood vessels surround the
anal canal and may be subject to enlargement and rup-
ture.

01001011101001101001001011101001101010

Orgone Machine Dynamic Recording.

File Spec. 4bbd.
Squat could stand on top of several piles of pallets.
Hemp rope wrapped against the skin of the neck that
four fingers could still fit through, just four.

Imposition of whole attractors on the body. It can be
liked to a virus - it hijacks and scrambles life codes
rather than replicating them wholesale.
The body is thin and sensitive, spent.
Days in white rooms then black rooms, sometimes lit,
other times not.
Identity and identity loss correspond to being or
slipping out of one's assigned category and the paths
through the social field associated with it; they are
the end effects, not the foundation, of the process of
individuation.

It's a movie but it's not.
Each scheduled stimulus takes its place in a growing
constellation of others 'like' it, to which there is
a correspondingly increased constellation of 'like'
responses.
He is dragged out onto the top of pallets. A crowd
gathers. If there is a way out of this impasse, it
will not lie in turning back.
The scenes are repeated over and over, replayed in a
thousand different variations.
This is the hanged man.
That is the hanged man.
Here is the hanged man.
There is the hanged man.
A pattern of repeated acts is a 'code' .
Getting hung ,and spurting, and the hangman moving in
and sucking it, and M coming up and MM coming up and
gobbling up his crotch just as his neck is being
snapped, and he's involuntarily coming — just as (sub-
ject) involuntarily comes when being screwed.
One is the image of the hangman and the other the image
of effect.
Covered in blood, broken but transfigured, and in
agreement with the world.
A trickle of saliva , or come, on someones lower lip.

File Spec. AM
'One thing is sure — he don't look good.'
'A filthy mess...'
'Sew her up, it's inoperable.'
'Clamps, nurse, he's bleeding like a pig.'
'Prepare the patient for a heart shot.'
'A round of drinks he dies on the table.'

0100101110100110100100101110100011010

Art and Calligraphy.

Nagual Art: one (subject's) late artistic pondering
(subject) took conception from Castanada book wherein
'Don Juan makes a distinction between the tonal universe and nagual. The tonal universe is the everyday
cause and effect universe, which is predictable

because it is pre-recorded. The nagual is the unknown,
the unpredictable, the uncontrollable'. Standard
beat-hippie fair still making 'mythical' distinctions
between one thing or another, using vague flightly
language, as if everything weren't connected completely, does not deal with otherness as (a)part of whole.
That everywhere is here, over there is here, always
here, and in this moment. The master of runes, the
secret action, under sound emergence words become bio-
morphized objects of desire acting as if things might
actually happen if you believe hard enough. 'Art' is
a lie and the writing finally becomes mere slight of
hand, not magic at all, but a trick, and a convenient
and repeatable one at that, an endlessly looping
advertisement for a culture of the Self.

0100101110100110100100101110100011010

Habit Love Scene.

Restoration, especially in the difficulies of anxiety
load, culled, unsightly tricks - (subject) wrote in
several places of pituitary associated drugs, he can
no longer recognize himself - instead - not only with
rage but in an ecstatic torment, in the virulence of
his own phantasms, existence itself shutters and
attains a level where there is nothing more than a hal-
lucinatory void, a dead foam mucus that clogs the
throat yellow green.

0100101110100110100100101110100011010

File Spec. 7 Sept. 1951: Mexico
Joan Adams, wife of (subject).
handwritten+

(subject) is sexist extreme, had advocated a complete
separation of the sexes and called 'love' a fraud per-
pertrated by the female sex.

Siti 1. First, claims 'accidentally' shot through

head by subject with pistol in a game of 'William
Tell'.
Siti 2. At close range missed the champagne glass bal-
anced on head. Wife dead. (see autopsy report)
Siti 3. Nex
Siti 5. (subject) jumps bail and returns to ut day
(subject) denies this story and instead claims that
loaded gun has dropped on kitchen table and misfired.
Siti 4. labeled 'pernicious foreigners' a free mur-
derer.

~~0100101110100110100100101110100011010~~

The following is the autopsy report for Burroughs (Vollmer), Joan.

Introduction

In this month of September, 1951, here in Mexico City
at the Desperation Mortuary, we are about to conduct
the autopsy of one Mrs. Joan Burroughs (nee Vollmer),
born 1924, common law wife of American tourist, Mr
William Burroughs. The Deceased was brought here with
a bullet hole in her forehead, seemingly caused by
fate, possible desperation - suicide, possession
escapism, control mania - murder, excessive, but fun-
induced alcohol/narcotics saturation - involuntary
manslaughter. This is a summary of the autopsy findings.

Case History

Mrs. B, 27 years old at the time of death, has been
in a relationship with Mr. Burroughs (37) for some
seven years, according to a small gathering of wit-
nesses at the scene of life extinguishment. Mr. Burroughs had been previously married to a German-Jewish
refugee, for the purpose of enabling the said
fraulein, emigration into the United States. Divorce

was completed in 1946. Mr. Burroughs has admitted that
he is a homosexual, but that the deceased was the only
woman with whom he has had a serious relationship. The
couple are said to have been happy, very casual, slept
separately, prone to playing suicidal games together,
and enjoyed rollicking fun discussions, with little
content of a personal nature, as well as excessive
bouts of drug taking and the drinking of alcoholic bev-
erages. Mrs. B. is survived by seven cats, a lizard
tree, a daughter, Julie (11) from a previous arrangement and a five year old son, Bill Junior, who has the
potential to display signs of drug addiction and cir-
rhosis of the liver. It is possible that Mrs. B's death
could become the inspiration, motivation and formula-
tion for Mr. Bs future and she could be afforded the
role of the Ugly
Spirit.

The deceased died of a bullet through the forehead,
dispatched there by Mr. Bs pistol. It is said that Mr.
B is a perfect marksman with a penchant for guns, which
he likes to display regularly, as well as his shoul-
der holster. Mr. B admits that he takes guns very seri-
ously and luckily, therefore Mrs. B died compassion-
ately.

Death occurred at the home of a friend of the deceased,
before an audience of a group of acquaintances (all
of whom have only been able to provide differing
accounts of the happening), when Mrs. B was coaxed by
Mr. B to balance a highball glass on top of her head
as part of their William Tell act. The distance between
Mr. and Mrs. B was six feet. Mr. B took the gun from
a suitcase, it was loaded and he shot. The missile
missed the glass and miraculously hit Mrs. B, one inch
lower, leaving most of her fine features and the
exquisite crystal glass of champagne intact until the
whole charade collapsed in a heap onto the linoleum -
clad floor seconds later. Mrs. B was taken to a near-
by hospital, where she died around one hour later.

Mr. B has apologized for his apparent error of judg-
ment, claiming his gun must have been faulty or that
his telepathic power to influence others, convinced
Mrs. B to move her head in order to protect the glass

in desperation. Mr. B has been arrested by the police, has been released from prison on bail, apparently waiting trial, but is likely to attempt an escape from Mexico. Mr. B would like to show his appreciation and gratitude to Joan for her timely death and the life-long struggle it has brought him, in his attempts to escape from possession. Yet another facet of life/death the couple seem to have shared.

External Examination

Some of the areas around the Os frontale, Os pari-etale, and the Os temporale have been left in virtu-ally perfect condition. There is a clean hole as though trepanned, in the Os frontale, with a larger, more ragged hole in the Os occipitale. The facial expres-sion is one of a response to grief, with the forehead thrown into furrows and the eyebrows are oblique, with the ends turned up, lusterless, like a death mask. The corners of the mouth turned down somewhat. The face clearly unused to smiling and virtually void of emo-tion, but with a clear look of intelligence. There are numerous needle marks to the skin of the body, more similar to that of a syringe, than pain relieving acupuncture. Traces of Vaseline around the vaginal and anal openings. Marijuana traces on the outer lips, cat scratch marks on the hands and legs. Traces of Lysol on hands. Disposition prior to death, clearly intoxi-cated with a paradox of manic experimentation and mis-ery. Unfortunately, no glass splinters in the head.

Internal Examination and Histology

Upon opening up the head, by cutting in a circular movement around the top of the skull, we find shat-tered bone fragments, dried blood spurts and traces of mangled connections. There is an over-abundance of enkephalin, a tiny peptide molecule, a natural opiate substance that is synthesized by the brain and acts like morphine to alleviate its own sensation of pain, demonstrating that the most fundamental aspect of our consciousness was present at point of death. Simi-larly there are traces of externally injected morphine, heroin, mescaline, opium marijuana and other drugs as well as large quantities of Oso Negro. The brain muscles are relaxed and the ventricle has collapsed to a flabby bag. The reticular formation in the stem of the brain, was implicated in the maintenance of consciousness as proof that the deceased was aware to the end of the likely outcome. This is consequent with the deceased, prior knowledge of the perpetrators manic obsession with control and need for freedom from possession. Proof of Mr. B's need for excessive influence is clear from an analysis of the cortex, which shows evidence of an incoming signal forewarning of the fatal event. Evidence that the mind may be suspended forever in the spirit of the perpetrator. The presence of a chemical transmitter between the terminations of one axon and the dendrites show that the deceased was in the act of communicating with Mr. B at the moment that life was being extinguished.

Discussion

The nature of death is clear. A bullet through the forehead. However, from the external and internal analysis, one can not be sure whether death was a deliberate shooting i.e. murder by Mr. B, who as a perfect marksman, would not normally miss from the range in question and has the motive of wishing to rid himself of a female companion, who was possibly over possessive; or has he claims, it was a monumental fatal accident, due to a fault with the gun. Similarly, we know that the Deceased was in a desperate state prior to death, somewhere between misery and ecstasy and was looking to release herself from the excessive influence and power mania of Mr. B, and as such may have deliberately moved her head into the firing line and committed suicide. The evidence shows that the couple were communicating at the point when the missile entered the forehead, leading to a suspicion that they were both conscious of the likely outcome. Or was it all just a drunken prank that went wrong. As Mr. B says: We have a destiny.

Dee, MD Fringecore Labs

List of Plates